DARK PSYCHOLOGY 101

*AN ESSENTIAL GUIDE TO LEARN PERSUASION
AND DARK PSYCHOLOGY TECHNIQUES AND HOW
TO READ AND INFLUENCE HUMAN BEHAVIOR TO
SPOT AND STOP MANIPULATION*

RAY BENEDICT

Tables of Contents

Part 1 Manipulation 6

Introduction 6

What Is Manipulation 11

Manipulation In Depth..24

Types Of Manipulation..39

Deal With Manipulation 46

Causes Of Manipulation 53

How To Analyze And Manipulate People 64

Techniques Of Dark Psychology And Dark Manipulation......80

How To Talk 95

Conversational Skills Techniques...................................*105*

Secrets of Persuasive People, How to Stop And Spot Manipulation..*118*

Be A Positive Influence On Others *129*

How To Defend Yourself From Manipulation....................*140*

Part 2 Persuasion *150*

Introduction *150*

Art Of Persuasion..*161*

Indicators That You're A Victim Of Manipulation.............*173*

How To Defend Yourself Against Emotional Predators *187*

Mind Control Methods...*201*

How To Influence People And Human Behavior...............*215*

Emotional Persuasion: What Is?...................................*228*

Conversational Skills Techniques.................................. *241*

Best Practices: The Optimization of Persuasion.............. *254*

Ethical Use... *269*

Conclusion *282*

Part 1 Manipulation

Introduction

Psychological warfare has been around for thousands of years. It has been used to instill fear in the enemy, create high or low morale, to intimidate, or even to inspire whole nations and mobilize soldiers. The best and effective kinds of psychological warfare is when the target doesn't even realize it. From Ancient civilizations to the Cold War, to the War on Terror. Psychological warfare has used techniques and tools based on the study of human behavior and thinking. The brain can be a powerful weapon and a weakness if properly manipulated both in and offensive and defensive way.

You may have also seen some techniques or practices a person in your life has used on you or others.

When looking over certain accounts of archetypical people who use certain techniques or practices, could you relate because you have used the same techniques? Maybe, you have realized that you may have been taken advantage of by someone who has used these techniques on you. If you feel surprised, excited or even guilty, you are not alone. Its purpose was to give you a rounded introduction into the realm of the study of dark psychology, techniques used in dark psychology, how to use some of these techniques and how to defend yourself for practitioners. It was only a taste of what dark psychology is.

Some of us have certain aspects of these skills or techniques ingrained in our lives and it has dictated our thoughts, actions and behaviors, we have in most cases readily used these skills from time to time. Some of us didn't realize that we are a "triangulator", "blaster", or a "projector", maybe even a "flirt". At the time we used some of the techniques. At the time, using them just seemed natural, as though it was instinctual. For some of us, these skills are as natural to us as breathing. Certain techniques may have become habitual through experiences in our environment, such as watching people close to us like a family member, friend or a significant other. Perhaps we saw a person we would consider a role model or a celebrity we admire use the exact same technique.

As human beings, we can have a need to feel a certain level of contentment. It is through this contentment that we can feel comfortable. We can feel this urge to find this contentment while at home, at school, or at work. When people, places or things impede on that contentment, we will react. Sometimes, we will learn from these situations or events on how to react the following time something impedes on our contentment again, either emotionally or methodically. Our behaviors and thoughts, as

well as how we react to them can be no different as how an animal reacts in the wild: A skunk, when feeling agitated, lifts its tail and shoots out an unpleasant liquid.

A bear will stand on its hind legs when it is ready to attack. For humans this is no difference.

You may have read about certain personality traits that use some of these dark psychological techniques, such as the narcissist or Machiavellian and related to some of their actions or behaviors.

If you feel guilty or upset, please try not to feel bad. We may have behaviors that are triggered when certain current experiences have mirrored others from our past.

Some of our behaviors and reactions are natural to keep us safe such as recoiling from a hot stove or feeling slightly uneasy when we are on top of a building looking down. Others are learned and can be directly linked to our past.

It is up to us whether or not we want to make these thoughts or behaviors go away or reinforce them.

Suppose you would like to know how to use these techniques in your personal life for you own gain. We are ambitious by nature. Like was stated earlier, we all want to feel a sense of comfort and contentment in our world. Maybe you want more than what is considered enough for contentment. Envy and jealousy can be powerful motivational feelings. Suppose you may want to get into management at your office, want to build up your confidence in a conversation or debate, or maybe you want to attract that special someone you have had your eye on and want to get and keep their attention.

Maybe you really want to be the "alpha" and be feared and respected by your colleagues and friends. You may want to achieve your goals by any means.

As we have seen, the study of human psychology and the term "dark psychology" is very broad and has many interpretations about its areas of study.

The internet, much like any informative resource, comes with an almost subconscious "buyers beware" warning label. While there are many experienced and dedicated researchers, there are also people who claim to have working experience and have their own experiences and theories in dark psychology, particularly in manipulative and persuasive techniques. While everyone is certainly entitled to their own opinion and experience when it comes to this field of study, it is up to you, to form your own opinion and experiences should you choose to continue researching dark psychology.

What Is Manipulation

Manipulation is a form of social influence which uses indirect, underhanded, and deceptive tactics to change people's perceptions and their resultant behavior. Usually, the end goal is to advance the interests of the person who initiates the manipulation. In many cases, manipulation happens at the expense of the person that is being manipulated; they may be emotionally, mentally, or physically harmed, or they may end up taking actions that are against their own best interests.

It's important to note that social influence is not inherently bad; one person can use manipulation techniques for the good of the person he or she is manipulating. For example, your family members or friends can use social influence and manipulation to get you to do something for your own good. The people who mean you well might manipulate you as a way of helping you deal with certain challenges or to help you make the right decisions.

We are more interested in the kind of manipulation that is done with malicious intentions. This is the kind of manipulation that disregards a person's right to accept or reject influence. It is coercive in nature; when the person being targeted tries to push against it, this kind of manipulation gets more sophisticated, and the end goal is to negate the person's will to assert for themselves.

How Manipulation Works

There are several psychological theories that explain how successful manipulation works. The first and perhaps the most universally accepted theory is one that was put forth by renowned psychologist and author, George Simon. He analyzed the concept of manipulation from the point of view of the manipulator, and he can up with a pattern of behavior that sums up every manipulation scenario. According to Simon, there are three main things that are involved in psychological manipulation.

First, the manipulator approaches the target by concealing his or her aggressive intentions. Here, the manipulator seeks to endear himself to his target without revealing the fact that his ultimate plan is to manipulate him or her. The manipulator accomplishes this by modifying his behavior and presenting himself as a good-natured and friendly individual, one who relates well with the target.

Secondly, the manipulator will take time to know the victim. The purpose of this is to get to understand the psychological vulnerabilities that the victim may have so as to figure out which manipulation tactic will be the most effective when he ultimately decides to deploy them.

Depending on the scenario, and the complexity of the manipulation technique, this stage may take anywhere between a few minutes to several years. For example, when a stranger targets you, he may take only a couple of minutes to "size you up" but when your partner or colleague seeks to manipulate you, he or she may spend months or even years trying to understand how your mind works.

The success of this second step depends on how well the first step is executed. If the manipulator successfully hides his intentions from you, he is in a better position to learn your weaknesses because you will instill some level of trust in him, and he will use that trust to get you to let down your guard and to reveal your vulnerabilities to him.

Thirdly, having collected enough information to act upon, the manipulator will deploy a manipulation technique of his choosing. For this to work, the manipulator needs to be able to marshal a sufficient level of ruthlessness; this means that the manipulation technique chosen will depend on what the manipulator can stomach. A manipulator with a conscience may try to use methods that are less harmful to manipulate you. One that completely lacks a conscious may use extreme methods to take advantage of you. Either way, manipulative people are willing to let harm befall their victims, and to them, the resultant outcome (which is usually in their favor) justifies the harm they cause.

Simon's theory of manipulation teaches us the general approach that manipulators use to get what they want from their victims, but it also points out something extremely important: Manipulation works, not just because of the actions of the manipulator, but also because of the reactions of the victims.

In the first step, the manipulator misrepresents himself to the victim: If the victim is able to see through the veil that the manipulator is wearing, the manipulation won't be successful. In the second step, the manipulator collects information about victims to learn about his or her vulnerabilities. The victim can be may be able to stop the manipulation at this stage by treating the manipulator's prying nature with a bit of suspicion. In the third stage, the manipulator uses coercive or underhanded techniques to get what he wants from the victim. Even in this stage, the victim may have certain choices on how to react to the manipulator's machinations.

The point here is that when it comes to manipulation, it takes two to tango. By understanding both the victim's and the manipulator's psychology, it's possible to figure out how you can avoid falling victim to other people's manipulation, and it can also help you become more conscientious so that you don't unknowingly use manipulation techniques on other people around you.

Let's look at the vulnerabilities that manipulators like to exploit in their victims.

The first and most prevalent vulnerability is the need to please others. We all have this need to some extent; we seek to please the people in our lives as well as total strangers. This is technically a positive quality that helps us coexist in our societies, but to manipulators, it's a weapon that can be used against you.

Many of us are willing to endure certain levels of discomfort just to make other people feel happy; we feel a certain sense of obligation towards one another, and that's just human nature. The closer we are to certain people, the greater the need to please them. For example, the need to please your friend is higher than your need to please a stranger.

Manipulators understand this, and they use it against their victims all the time. If a manipulator wants to get something big out of you, he will first take the time to get closer to you, not just to get to know your vulnerability, but also to increase the sense of obligation you feel towards him.

The second vulnerability is the need for approval and acceptance. Again, as social beings, we all have an innate desire to feel accepted. We want people to love us, to think of us as members of their groups, and to choose us over other people. This feeling can be addictive, and it can give other people (especially manipulative ones) a lot of power over us. The vast majority of manipulation victims are people who have close personal relationships with the manipulators; in other words, they have an emotional need to gain the acceptance or approval of the manipulator. The remaining manipulation victims can be manipulated because they want to be a part of something (a group, a social class, etc.).

The third vulnerability that manipulators like to exploit is what psychologists refer to as "emetophobia" (which is the fear of negative emotions). To some extent, we are all afraid of negative emotions; we will do lots of things to avoid feeling angry, afraid, stressed, frustrated, and worried, etc. We want to lead happy and fulfilled lives, and anything that makes us feel "bad" is a threat to that sense of fulfillment. So, in many cases, we will do what manipulators want if it serves to alleviate that "bad" feeling. Manipulators know this, and they use negative emotions against us all the time.

The fourth vulnerability is the lack of assertiveness. Assertiveness is a very rare quality; even people who you may generally consider to be assertive are likely to cave in if manipulators push hard enough. Even when you are willing to stand your ground and to say "No," manipulators can be very persistent, and in the end, they can wear you out.

The fifth vulnerability is the lack of a strong sense of identity. Having a strong sense of identity means having clear personal boundaries, and understanding one's own values. Unfortunately, these qualities aren't so strong in most of us, and that leaves us open to manipulation. Manipulators succeed by pushing our boundaries little by little, making them blurry, and then taking control of our identities.

Finally, having an external locus of control, and having a low level of self-reliance are also key vulnerabilities that manipulators love to exploit. When you have an external locus of control, it means that your identity and your sense of self are external to you. It means you view yourself through other people's eyes. It means that you are extrinsically motivated. When you have low self-reliance, it means you depend on other people for sustenance and for emotional stability. It means that if support systems in your life are taken away, you can easily find yourself leaning on a manipulator, which leaves you at his mercy.

Manipulation is a Part of Human History

Looking at history, we will see that some of our most loved historical figures practiced manipulation. During the founding of the United States, our founding fathers had to use socio-political manipulation to help set a revolution in motion. By first using various economic manipulation tactics on the other colonies and colonists that joining their cause would benefit them more than say the British. Secondly, among each other many political games had to be played, all using subterfuge and manipulation to help get the right people in place to lead the country.

Manipulation had to be used in its persuasive form here so that the right person could get the right backing. This was not evil nor bad; it showed how the covert tactic of playing into a willing pawns card could allow for everyone involved to win. Imagine, too, that they had to manipulate the British for quite a while before things truly were sent into emotion. They had to manipulate them into trusting and believing them. These same kinds of manipulative games have been used for good by many great figures in history to simply manipulate their opposition into doing what is right.

Think of the rallies and marches during the civil rights movement. It did so much good by manipulating and playing on people's emotions and wants for a just society. This is not malicious manipulation, but more so an evil required to enact great change in this world.

Knowing that manipulation is not always an evil wantonly committed for evil makes it much easier to understand the kind of tactics people will use. In a big part complimenting and persuading someone through charisma is, in a sense, manipulation. You are telling them what they want to hear whether it compliments or being a shoulder to cry on for someone.

Almost every friendship that is healthy has this give and take. For a large part, these are simple altruistic forms of manipulation that allow and help both sides win and accomplish a goal of theirs. Charisma and persuasion two topics I mentioned earlier. Persuasion and charisma are the simplest forms of human manipulation.

Manipulators work by making someone come across as if they are the type of person who loves and cares about you and would drop anything if need be to help you with something. This glib or charm is a manipulative tactic that one could use for themselves to try and gain friends. Once again, there is nothing wrong with this; its more in line with gaming the system. You are putting on a front that people want, and as a result of this, they then become drawn to you easier and wish to spend time with you or do stuff to you.

This is a simple day to day manipulation that we all do – whether we realize it or not. This type of manipulation on a social scale is not for harm, but for companionship. Have you ever heard the expression "a little white lie"?

The issue is that the word makes manipulation sound bad and evil. But the truth is that by doing simple things that social charmer does, like mirroring body language, buying someone food, or always asking about their interests and ignoring yours is basic human interaction. You can get people to trust you and even help you get ahead in life, especially if this kind of interaction is taking place in the social world.

Manipulation and Success

You could argue that to a certain degree without some powerful people in society who used manipulation to get their way to the top, the world would fall apart. Maybe we would not be so successful. This kind of manipulation is far more different than the much more sinister mind manipulation. It is simple to understand the term mental manipulation. Simply put, mental manipulation occurs with the nefarious act of playing mind games, such as making you feel guilty for not buying or doing something, getting you to question your own judgment.

This covert manipulative behavior can become so common that we oftentimes don't recognize it until it is too late by which point, we have befallen the consequences of said manipulation. Avoiding these consequences is a great thing to be capable of doing. But it can be hard to avoid if you are not sure what you are avoiding. Well, that is why it is good to know what mental manipulation is due to its subtlety. It is this type of manipulation – mental manipulation – which is perhaps the most common form of manipulation you will encounter in your day to day life.

Mental manipulation shows its face a lot in relationships with friends or other people you care about. As a result, the people who do this are very good at it and hide it well. Besides being such a common form of manipulation people will use, it is important to realize that there are many varieties of mental manipulation to which you could easily find yourself as a victim.

Consider times when you are speaking with a group of friends, and one person tries to make you feel guilty due to you making a choice to not buy them an extremely expensive gift for their birthday. They then might try mental manipulation to get you to fall for the trap of "oh well, I have done all these things for you; do you not think it is fair if you get me xyz."

Behavior like this is where manipulation becomes evil and unacceptable. This is not trying to sway someone over to your side of thinking for a good reason or trying to survive in a time of crisis. This narcissistic person is using manipulation to hurt people, and that is never acceptable.

Understanding the subtle moral differences in manipulation makes it easier for you to appreciate how to learn about different manipulative tactics as a whole and how you yourself can go about defending from and using them as well as giving you the useful ability of knowing how to avoid people who could potentially try and manipulate you in person, this includes the media and everything else we see. Since they all use manipulation tactics, understanding this is half the battle.

Manipulation In Depth

How would you feel if you never realized that all along you had been used as a pawn? Or that you've been acting out someone else's script? The realization that you have never been entirely in charge of your life or actions, in general, can crush you. It sounds scary. This is essentially what emotional manipulation is about. People usually toss the word emotional manipulation in regular conversations, but they seldom know what it truly means. Thus, it is quite essential to understand what emotional manipulation entails and to set the record straight. Emotional manipulation is a psychological or social means by which an individual who might be wise, or at least thinks he is, influences your behavior or responses to a situation or issue in a manner that isn't true to yourself intending to satisfy his needs or wants.

You might think you're still yourself because you don't realize you're acting out someone else's script. Their approach doesn't always have to be forceful, but it certainly plays your psyche to their beat. Manipulation is exploitative and can cripple you with self-doubt. It is about someone else using what truly covertly belongs to you to fulfill all their desires without obtaining your permission to do so. The main issue isn't about the secrecy involved, but about the fact that manipulators can make you do things you might have not commonly done.

Tactics of Covert Manipulation

A lot of people are unaware of the fact that manipulators are continually trying to confuse and control them. You might have experienced a feeling of uneasiness because the manipulator's words don't match his actions, or you might feel like you're being forced to accept a specific request even though it feels like a demand. The way people react usually tends to escalate the degree of abuse and essentially encourages them to play into the hands of the manipulator. All this can make the person being manipulated start to feel guilty or even small.

If you're dealing with a manipulator, then the phrase, "know your enemy" is something you must be aware of. You must be able to spot any red flags and respond strategically to the covert tactics of manipulation. By understanding what the manipulator is up to, it puts you in a better position to protect yourself. You cannot defend yourself if you're not aware of what is happening. If someone is behaving passive-aggressively towards you, it is known as covert aggression. The extent of consciousness or unconsciousness of a manipulator's behavior is debatable. From a victim's perspective, it never matters, because the effect happens to be the same. If you display any empathy towards the manipulator, it is the risk of being mistreated in the future increases drastically. Regardless of whether the manipulator's attack on you is overt or covert, it is known as aggression.

If you are unaware of the tactics which manipulators use, it will be quite challenging to break free from their spell or hold over you. You may be deceiving yourself that you are in charge of your life and actions, even when you are not. Emotional manipulation is often seen in a bad light, but there are times when you might need to use it to get what you need from individuals who wouldn't cooperate with you initially. By being aware of the various tactics of manipulation, you cannot only prevent yourself from being manipulated but can also take corrective action if you're being manipulated. Emotional manipulators often work on the weak points in the victim's psyche and use the same to make themselves feel better.

It is a widespread belief that most of the covert

manipulators say or do things intentionally to get whatever they desire. The two things a covert manipulator wants more than anything else are power and control. The apparent goal of any form of manipulation is to influence others to meet one's needs. However, chronic manipulators often do this to get control and power over others. They maintain their domination over others through constant and recurring emotional manipulation and emotional abuse. They are often passive-aggressive and might lie, act like the injured party or even pretend surprise if you complain about their behavior. Any criticism aimed towards them can be easily turned against you. If you are wondering why a manipulator acts the way he does, then you aren't alone. They usually do this for the following reasons.

- To make your defensive or to lower your guard

- To avoid any form of confrontation

- To trigger self-doubt in their target

- To make you question your judgment along with your perception of reality

- To brush away any responsibility

- To hide their manipulative nature or ulterior motives

- To avoid changing their behavior

Being subjected to manipulation can make you lose your trust in yourself and have you doubting everything you feel and perceive. Some forms of aggression, like blatant criticism and narcissistic abuse, are quite common. However, there are other subtle forms of emotional manipulation or abuse like complaining, denial, feigning ignorance, shifting blame, lying, emotional blackmail, and insincere flattery which are less noticeable. The techniques employed by emotional predators are varied and numerous.

Lying

A habitual liar is someone who is used to lying all the time, even when it isn't required. They don't lie because they are guilty or afraid, but they do this intending to try to confuse you. By confusing you, they take away your ability to make rational decisions and making you easy to manipulate to get what they want. Some manipulators use accusations along with other manipulative tactics to make you defensive. Lying doesn't always have to be direct. Indirect means of lie include the omission of specific information or providing vague information.

Absolute denial

Lying and denial tend to go hand in hand. The tactic of denial used by emotional predators is not unconscious, unlike the one where the victims of abuse don't realize they are being abused. Another example of unconscious denial is an addict who doesn't know he has an addiction. Whenever an emotional predator employs denial, he is quickly disavowing any promises he has made or denying the knowledge about such signs, behavior, or even arguments. The manipulator might also try to minimize and rationalize his behavior by coming up with excuses. Don't be surprised if the manipulator attempts to make it seem like you're making a big deal out of a tiny issue or tries to rationalize his actions by making you question your judgment. He might even come up with various excuses to gain your sympathy. Once you give in, you are sinking deeper into his manipulative trap.

Avoid confrontations

A manipulator never likes to accept his faults or shoulder his responsibilities. He doesn't like taking responsibility for his actions or words. He will try to avoid confrontation at all costs. If you notice that someone is continuously avoiding any discussions about their behavior or is refusing to discuss it, it is a tactic of manipulation. Not only will he avoid a confrontation, but he will also try shifting the blame onto you. Since a manipulator knows he can control you, the possibility of an encounter can prompt a response like "stop harping on me," "don't be such a nag," or "you are a fault-finding machine." Mostly the manipulator is trying to shift the blame onto you. Avoidance doesn't always have to be apparent; it can be subtle. A manipulator can subtly change the topic of discussion to take the spotlight away from himself. Or he might try flattering you or giving you compliments to take the focus away from the issue. Emotional abusers might say things like, "You know how much I love you," to lower your defenses. Once he succeeds, you might not even remember why you were upset to begin with.

By being evasive, an emotional predator blurs the facts and confuses you by planting seeds of self-doubt. A manipulator becomes slightly uncomfortable when you point out any inconsistencies in his stories and might even claim that you aren't compatible together. A skilled manipulative liar hates it when others question his stories and half-truths. In fact, he might quickly shift the blame onto you and make you doubt your judgment.

Shame and guilt

Another common tactic employed by emotional predators

is projection. It's a defensive tactic wherein the manipulator starts accusing others of his actions or behaviors. Remember the saying, "the best defense is a great offense?" Well, the manipulator is primarily using this tactic by shifting the blame onto his victim. By doing this, he is putting you on the defensive. The manipulator shrugs off any responsibility for his actions and stays innocent while you are now left to deal with any shame or guilt you experience. A manipulator is fully aware of his victim's style of thinking and will use this knowledge against the victim. An abuser will come up with ways to blame others and his victims instead of apologizing for his behavior. This is quite similar to the way a criminal uses a defense of police incompetence to shift the blame onto others. A partner who is aggressive and resorts to physical violence might blame his spouse for his behavior. By moving the responsibility onto others and making their victims feel guilty, they are gaining control and power over the victim.

By guilt-tripping you and shaming you, he is essentially gaining power over you. So, the worse you feel, the better it is for the manipulator. He might even act like a martyr and say he deserves better after all that he has done for you. This can be coupled with harsh criticism that you are ungrateful or even selfish. Shaming is not just about making you feel guilty, but it is also about triggering feelings of inadequacy. By demeaning you, he is making himself feel better. For instance, a manipulator will effectively shift the blame onto his victims by suggesting everything is their fault and not his. For example, "we would have had a happy relationship if you would just believe me and stop being paranoid." At times, spouses might compare their existing relationship with a prior connection to make their current partner feel inferior and weak.

The best way to blame the victim is by using guilt and shame. For instance, even if you find concrete evidence on your partner's phone, suggesting that he's cheating on you, the manipulator will find a way to turn this against you. Instead of coming clean about his indiscretion, he might act like you are violating his privacy or that you had no right to check his phone. He might also act like the victim or say you don't trust him. He is essentially taking away the focus from his indiscretion and is now concentrating on your actions by blaming you; your partner has successfully avoided a confrontation about his cheating. In the end, you, the actual victim in the situation, will start to feel guilty about your actions. You might also feel like your anger is no longer justified or valid. He is invalidating your feelings while getting away with his misdeeds.

Intimidation

Intimidation can be mental as well as physical and doesn't always come in the form of direct threats. It can also be in the form of statements like, "I am well-connected and have friends in high places," "you aren't as young as you once were," or "have you considered the consequences of your decision?" Another strategy commonly employed by manipulators is to come up with fictitious stories told to provoke fear in their victims. A manipulator uses his victim's anxiety to get what he desires - a sense of absolute control.

Magnification

While dealing with a manipulator, he will often magnify his problems while diminishing the intensity of your questions. This is usually done quite subtly so that you don't even realize that you're being manipulated. For instance, if you bring up a problem with any trauma you faced in childhood, a manipulative partner will point out that he never even had parents to begin with. Initially, it might seem like the manipulator is sympathizing with you, but effectively he is just diminishing your problems. By doing this, he is trying to make you feel like your problems are not worth pondering over or even discussing.

Aggressive jokes

It might seem like the manipulator is joking, but here's sneakily engaging in offensive jokes which demean you as a person. Often, the manipulator will joke about any insecurities you have or any issues you are struggling with. This is done to overpower you. Don't be surprised if the manipulator or partner starts joking about any trauma you suffered in life. For instance, joking about a failed marriage is not funny, but this doesn't prevent the manipulator from doing so. Mostly, he is trying to hurt you but is doing so by masquerading the insult in the form of a joke or sarcasm. So, if you do react towards it, you will come across as being extremely touchy about an issue, which he must not have even joked about, to begin with.

Name-calling

A manipulator often believes that he is right when others are always wrong. He will go to any extent to prove that he is right. If you're not thick-skinned, then you cannot deal with the kind of criticism a manipulator doles out. You can feel quite annoyed and even rejected once someone starts calling you an extremist, a troublemaker, or even an idiot. A manipulator will resort to name-calling to overpower you. Once you begin to feel bad about yourself, you become incredibly vulnerable to manipulation.

Smear campaign

Gossiping and indulging in smear campaigns are two things a manipulator will never shy away from. Gossip can be quite harmful when left unchecked. It is not beneath a manipulator to spread vicious rumors about you. He does all this to make others think ill about you. All the vile stories he covers will undoubtedly harm your equation with others.

Triangulation

In this technique, the manipulator will try to validate his wrongdoings or wrong acts towards you by making you question someone else instead of the manipulator himself. The manipulator might be mentally abusive towards you and the moment you react to it by letting him know that such behavior isn't acceptable to you, they will conveniently direct your attention to what someone else is doing. For instance, if you complain about the mistreatment he's doling out, he might point out that another friend of yours is perfectly fine when her partner mistreats her. By doing this, he is distracting you while making you feel like you're overreacting.

All these tactics can cripple your self-confidence and kill your identity as an individual. You can forgive and move on, but never forget. If you turn a blind eye toward it, the manipulation will continue. After a while, you will be riddled with trauma, and your self-worth will take a massive blow. The first step to dealing with manipulation is to become aware of the problem.

Why Is Manipulation Undesirable

Perhaps the most apparent reason why manipulation is considered to be genuinely undesirable is that it is morally wrong. Apart from this, it also harms the person being manipulated. This harm can be emotional, mental, or even physical at times. For instance, an advertisement glorifying the purchase and use of cigarettes is manipulative. It is worshiping something, which is detrimental to one's health. Manipulation uses tactics that are usually considered to be immoral or, at best, dodgy. It is quintessential that we all treat one another as rational beings instead of objects to be played with. Manipulation is often carried on to gain undue advantage over others to fulfill the needs of the manipulator. Therefore, it is safe to say that manipulation is selfish. Various tactics employed by the manipulator tend to take away the victim's freedom to choose. So, essentially, the manipulator is forcing his victims to do something, regardless of whether they want to or not. Manipulation is also quite similar to lying. The manipulator is always in control of his victim's behavior and thinking. Manipulation can also harm the victim's sense of self, self-esteem, and self-confidence.

Types of Manipulators

There are different types of manipulators, and each of them tends to use a specific technique to manipulate their targets.

Perhaps the most common type of manipulator you will ever come across is the one who makes you feel guilty. Nothing can make you feel worse than an unnecessary guilt trip. If you don't comply with the demands of the manipulator, he will make you feel guilty about it. Even if it were right to deny his claim, the manipulator would do everything he possibly can to make you feel bad.

A masked braggart tends to make his target feel inferior or inadequate covertly. These kinds of manipulators are well aware of the fact that he will look proud and presumptuous, not to mention arrogant if he always brags about his accomplishments. He is worried that others will think of him as being bold. However, he indeed loves bragging about his accomplishments, and he goes about doing this differently. For instance, this kind of manipulator will never call his victim fat, but will instead say, "My small size shirts are so baggy now," even when he knows his victim wears XL. By belittling his victim, he is boasting about his accomplishments.

Types Of Manipulation

Many of us are aware that manipulation is a form of deceit. Manipulators are the people who use deceptive tactics to achieve what they want, but this is regardless of the consequences to those around them, particularly to the victims of their tactics.

Manipulators are not worried about how their manipulation will affect you personally or psychological damage that they inflict; all they care about is getting the results that they want. These results could be anything from getting to pick the restaurant to getting access to the funds or gifts needed to perpetuate a particular social standing.

Knowing the warning signs is a start, but knowing the type of emotional manipulator you are dealing with can also help you in defending yourself against them and their deceptive tactics. So let's talk about the various types of manipulators out in the world, thus gaining a more complete understanding of how they operate to achieve their ends.

Indifferent

First up is the indifferent manipulator, which is the one that acts like they don't care. These manipulators often seem indifferent towards anything you are doing or saying. This indifference is not just toward your actions, but any circumstances in your life, including difficulties or even celebrations.

In acting indifferent, these individuals have actually caught your attention. You spend time and energy attempting to achieve that breakthrough to capture their attention, thus hoping to achieve a deeper connection. However, they have already singled you out for some specific reason, so they will provide just enough interest to keep you hooked without really breaking out of the indifferent cycle.

In fact, the more indifferent they act, the more questions you are going to ask because you genuinely care. However, when you start asking questions that is when the manipulation starts in an earnest fashion, because now a manipulator can use that they have information provided through those conversations to dig their hooks in ever deeper. Without them having to do or say anything directly, they have begun to play on your heart strings, thus achieving the goal of your personal emotional investment into their lives.

As the victim, you are now in a position that allows them to use your sympathy to "make them feel better", but in reality, the manipulator is now just starting their sting to take from their victims whatever they want, from the emotional to the material. But when the victim has nothing left, then the manipulator moves on to their following victim, typically without any real remorse.

Still at this moment, you are still a goose to be fleeced, so the indifferent manipulator may also take advantage of another type of manipulator, which is the one that is always in distress or poor me.

Poor Me

This particular type of manipulator may be the easiest to spot, but in combination with other traits, makes them easy to fall for over and over again. So, what do the poor me manipulators do so effectively when dealing with their victims?

The poor me manipulators use sympathy and guilt, appealing to their victims need to try to help another human being in trouble or assist someone out of a sense of charity or faith. Appealing to their victim's better nature is one consistent way that a manipulator will attempt to get into someone's head. Often it is this goodness that a manipulator can turn on their victim.

It is simply part of our human nature to feel for people who are struggling through something or who are facing various challenges different from the ones that we are facing. We react by doing what we can to help them out, so we tend to cater to their demands without realizing we are being manipulated.

The demands can at first appear reasonable, but over time, will simply grow in complexity. These requests quickly turn into commands and ones that often prove to be real time suckers. Thus, your whole world suddenly becomes completely focused on the manipulator. So the isolation can begin, making it harder for you or loved ones to observe the manipulation and point it out to you.

Critic

As with other manipulators, this particular type is a bit more aggressive than the first two types. They will actively focus on their victim's habits and emotional cues. After finding areas of sensitivity or weakness, the manipulator will begin to focus on them, subtlety at first, and then gradually growing bolder over time.

While it might be easy to spot what a manipulator is doing, many of us who fall victim to manipulators are helpless to stop it, unless we work on improving our mindset. Other ways to help avoid being a victim or getting out of a manipulative situation involve using anti-manipulation techniques.

The critic uses criticism as a way to get what they want because the victim is trying to please, although the critical manipulator will set a bar for their standards, which the victim will find impossible to meet. The constant criticism for their victim contributes to neither making them feel like they are not good enough nor will they ever be good enough. Through manipulation the critic makes you feel like you are worthless and they are better than you.

Thus, to achieve a better sense of your own self-worth, the victim will attempt to be more like the critic or to do things just the way the critic prefers them. Personality changes may also occur, because the victim just wants to gain the affection and praise of the critic. However, the victim does not know this goal is simply unachievable.

Still as bad as these types of manipulators can prove to be, there is one that can be far worse. Why? Because they are willing to go much further than any of the others to achieve their goals, including using fear and violence.

Intimidators

When this particular manipulator comes into play, the victim can be in a very dangerous place. These manipulators are the worst of the worst; they are even more aggressive than the critic. In fact, the intimidator is not just critical, but they use fear and violence to make their victims cower.

These manipulators are more familiar with the stick, than using a more carrot like approach. Once their victim is afraid, these manipulators can easily have their demands met. In abusive relationships with intimidators, the tactic of using anger comes out frequently, along with the need to punish. Both of these tactics play into the fear aspect of the intimidator.

Let's face it, when we are afraid of someone, as individuals we tend to give in much quicker than if we felt in a position of power or a defendable position. These manipulators are all about stripping away any sense of being able to defend yourself, physically or psychologically.

Nobody dares stand up to a person who uses fear to manipulate them because they are literally afraid of what that person might physically do. This is where the manipulator uses violence or the threat of violence to complete their hold on the victim. Abusive spousal relationships often demonstrate this type of intimidation manipulation with a mix of violence all too well.

So now that we have a greater understanding of the manipulator, their types and tactics, it's time to get a better understanding of the victim. However, you might be the one displaying those traits.

So what specifically about your personality or way of carrying yourself is sending up flags for a manipulator to zero in on?

Deal With Manipulation

Psychological manipulation is always going to be a very loaded and heavy-handed issue. It can often be referred to as lying, deceiving, skewing, distorting, gaslighting, intimidating, guilting, and other such things. Manipulators can also take the form of many different people over the course of your life. Sometimes, the person who is manipulating you might be a parent, sibling, boss, classmate, coworker or romantic partner, among others. That's why manipulation is such a complex topic to handle. It can take the form of various tactics, and it can also be employed by various agents. This is why it can be increasingly difficult for someone to be able to identify and deal with a manipulative person.

You were exposed to the many different feelings, sensations, and experiences that you might have should you ever find yourself in a manipulative relationship environment. As long as you keep your eyes peeled and you make an active effort in seeking these red flags out, it shouldn't really be a problem. Now, it's a matter of dealing with these people and managing their advances.

First evaluate whether the person is more of a systematic or unconscious manipulator. The more systematic, profound manipulators are almost certainly beyond reach. They can have grand visions and don't care who they have to get by to pursue their goals, they may simply enjoy controlling others, perhaps they have had childhood traumas and issues that lead them to exploit others for fulfillment. These types of people are more aware of it and aggressively pursue their manipulative traits. Whatever the case may be, if possible, keep your distance on these types of people. Indeed, the easy solution would be to cut this person out of your life, right? It can be so easy to just burn bridges with someone if you know that they have manipulative tendencies and that they would be so willing to advance their own personal interests at your expense. That kind of selfishness should warrant a cutting of ties. However, it's not always going to be that simple. There are going to be times when the person who is manipulating you is someone you have a deep bond and connection with. There is even a chance they are not consciously aware of their behavior themselves. For instance, if your parent, partner or friend is manipulating you, it's not going to be so easy to just break that relationship off entirely. This is especially true if you love your parents and you know that they love you in return. In this case, it's not just a matter of eliminating a manipulative person from your life. Rather, it becomes an issue of managing this individual.

When dealing with a manipulative person, it's very important that you tread lightly. Keep in mind that there is also a paternal kind of manipulation. They might not have bad intentions, and they might take offense to the fact that you are accusing them of being manipulative. That is why you have to be extra cautious and sensitive when you broach the issue with them.

First, Be Safe

If you know that you are in danger whenever you are with this manipulative individual in your life, always make sure that there is a third-party present. You can never really know what they might do to you if the two of you are alone. So, before you confront them about your manipulation, make sure that you have someone else in the room. You need that mediator; someone who would be able to help bridge the two of you. You can always call on a mutual friend, a shared loved one, or a trusted confidante. In more serious cases, you can even seek professional help from a licensed therapist. The point here is that the confrontation process should never be conducted recklessly. Your safety is always going to be the first priority here. And a lot of the time, that means having someone else in the room to be with you.

Take a Diplomatic Approach to Initiating a Dialogue

You can either choose to work your own influence on them to lessen the negative effects, or you could just confront them. The initial confrontation doesn't have to be so hot and impassioned. In fact, the best approach to confronting this individual would be to be as calm and collected as can be. You want to make sure that you are taking emotions out of the equation here. Keep in mind that a manipulative person is always going to capitalize on the emotionality of a person. If you take that ammo away from them, then it leaves them very little to work with. In addition to that, it's more likely that they won't react in such a hostile manner if you take a more civil approach to initiating this dialogue with them. Using people's own words against them makes it harder to resist whatever it is you are asking them to do, if one claims to be selfless, then they would not partake in certain actions to begin with.

You have to remember that starting the conversation

isn't always going to go so smoothly. It's very much likely that they will resist at first. However, you need to stay persistent. You have to emphasize the importance of this conversation. However, if they do decide to engage with you in this conversation, then you need to stay mindful of the following tips.

Don't Fight Back

If they are going to be hostile with you about it, resist the urge to fight back. You have to learn to pick your spots. Responding to them in a hostile manner is only going to result in you playing into their games. You don't want that. You want to make sure that you stay calm all throughout. When they get emotional, don't invalidate these feelings. Their emotions might actually be very authentic regardless of whether they are based on distorted truths or not. A person can still feel angry about something that is a complete lie or fantasy. Keep that in mind.

Instead of invalidating their feelings and telling them that they're being unreasonable, hear them out. With this method, you will get a chance to really understand them more. You will be able to gain insight into their behavioral triggers. The more you understand them, then the better it will be for you to manage this entire situation.

Set Clear Limits and Boundaries

Once you have heard their side of the tale, it's now time for you to air out your personal grievances. Again, you need to make sure that you keep emotions out of it. You don't want them to be invalidating what you're saying just because you're being hysterical. You want to be honest about it, and be straight. You shouldn't be beating around the bush anymore. Make sure that all of the skeletons come out of the closet. Be courteous, but also, don't pull any punches. No matter how uncomfortable it might be to speak honestly about your feelings, you're going to have to do so.

If you're interested in salvaging the relationship, then emphasize this point. Make sure they understand that you don't want to block them out of your life completely. However, you also need to emphasize that you will be setting clear limits and boundaries as you move forward in your relationship together. Make them understand that the integrity of your relationship is dependent on their respect for the boundaries that you set in it.

Know When It's Time to Walk Away

Sometimes, you just need to be able to know when it's

time to walk away. No matter how painful it is to cut yourself loose from someone who you love dearly, you still have to do so for the sake of your own well-being. You should not be making any room for toxicity or manipulative behavior that causes burden in your life regardless of who it might be coming from. At the end of the day, the only real person who has your back is yourself. That is why you have to make it a point to protect yourself at all costs. If there is no way for you to find a peaceful means of coexisting with one another that doesn't involve any form of harmful manipulation that is taking value out of your life, then you need to be able to walk away from that.

Granted, walking away from someone who is close to you isn't going to be a quick and easy process. It's going to be a very painful and gradual one. However, you always need to prioritize your own well-being above the relationships that you have with others, especially if they are the toxic and systematic type. Stay safe and guarded. No relationship is worth losing your sense of self over.

Causes Of Manipulation

Now that you are fairly competent in identifying emotional and covert manipulation tactics, let's understand what leads people to manipulate others. This may help you deal with them more efficiently.

We've all been victims of everything from pathological lying to being made to feel inadequate to suffering awful smear campaigns. They are beyond reasonable standards of human behavior. What makes people turn into sinister manipulators? What leads manipulators to use the tactics they do? What makes them defy norms of human behavior and turn to underhanded techniques to have their way with people?

Read on to get deeper insights about what makes people manipulate others in ways you'd never imagine.

Fear

Why does a person use manipulation to fulfill his/her own agenda? Simple - fear!

It is obvious that manipulators fear that they will never be able to gain the desired outcome on their own abilities.

That if they act ethically, people and life will not reward them positively. They operate from the view that people are life, and people are positioned against them. Manipulators fear everyone as their enemy and believe life will not necessarily be favorable to them if they act favorably.

There is a fear that resources are limited, and if they don't gain something, others will. They think it's a dog-eat-dog universe where people must be controlled to help them accomplish the desired result. This control can be in any form – emotional, psychological, financial or practical. They want to control people, so they can achieve their desired agenda and put their fear to rest.

Manipulators are constantly living under fear and insecurity. 'What if this doesn't happen?' 'What if my partner leaves me for someone else?' 'What if someone gains an upper hand over me?' They want to win and control all the time to combat an inherent sense of fear.

Where does this fear stem from? It originates from a deep sense of unworthiness. This simply translates as 'I am certainly not worthy of the good things and people in life, hence, these things and people will leave me. To prevent them from leaving me, I must resort to some underhanded techniques that will give me absolute control over the people and things I believe I don't deserve.' In short, the underlying message is – 'I am undeserving or unworthy of people and things!'

Low or No Conscience

Lack of conscience is another fundamental reason for manipulation. When a person fails to realize that he/she is responsible for their own reality, there is a greater tendency to operate without a conscience. Manipulators don't believe a fair system exists. Also, they've stopped evolving. They don't learn from earlier experiences or try to accomplish a state of congruence between inner emotions and external life.

They view manipulation as a safe or secure world for getting the desired result, despite the fact that these results have not brought them satisfaction in the past. Emotionally and psychologically, they keep coming back to square one from time to time, never learning their lesson. To avoid this lesson, they will create another reason to manipulate. Thus, they are caught in vicious circle of unworthiness or dissatisfaction, thus, creating another manipulation need.

Manipulation doesn't pay beyond the initial brief fix since the manipulative action is not authentic, balanced or effective. It is a defense reaction to perceived hurt, unworthiness, fear or insecurity. By being manipulative, the person is attempting to offset these emotions.

Manipulation is a deliberate act that is not aligned with a person's conscience or greater good. The person doesn't operate with a "we are one" understanding, which means he/she seeks to gain through manipulation by authenticity rather than non-authenticity. Anything gained through non-authenticity only leads to narrow victories, ongoing trouble, emptiness or fear and unworthiness. This creates an even bigger sense of unworthiness. Again, unworthiness is a fear of not being worthy of others' love and acceptance.

Manipulative folks do not learn, evolve or realize the power of authenticity. Lack of realization of the real power of authenticity and worthiness comes from knowing that one is cherished and accepted for what they really are. In essence, a feeling of unworthiness is often at the core of manipulation.

They Don't Want to Pay the Price Attached to Reach Their

Goals

People often manipulate to serve their needs because they do not want to pay the price attached to their goal. They often strive to accomplish the objective or serve their purpose without wanting to give back or pay the price in return.

For instance, if you don't want your partner to leave you, the relationship will take work. You'll have to give your partner love, compassion, understanding, time, loyalty, encouragement, inspiration, a secure future and much more.

A manipulator may not want his/her partner to leave them, but they don't want to pay the price of maintaining a happy, secure and healthy relationship, whereby the partner will never leave them. They may not want to be loyal or spend much time with their partner, and yet they expect them to stay. When people are not ready to pay the price of accomplishing what they want, they may resort to manipulation or underhanded techniques to achieve these goals without paying the price attached to them.

Similarly, if a manipulative person wants to be promoted in his/her workplace, rather than working hard, staying past work hours, upgrading their skills or getting a degree, they will simply manipulate their way into the position. The person is not prepared to pay the price or do what it takes to be promoted.

At times, it's deeply ingrained in a person's psyche that wants are bad or that he/she shouldn't have any desires since it makes them come across as selfish. Manipulation then becomes a way to get what they desire or need without even asking for it.

Manipulators realize there is a price attached to everything. A person won't do them a favor without expecting a favor in return. They won't keep getting things if they don't demonstrate kindness and gratitude. A person won't love them or have sex with them without getting commitment, loyalty and love in return. Manipulators try to push their luck by trying to get something without paying the price attached to it. It is often the easy way out.

They Think They Won't Get Caught

Another reason people manipulate is because they think they can get away with their sneaky acts and that the victims won't realize they are being manipulated. They are also confident that the victim can't do anything even if their manipulation cover is blown.

What gives manipulators the feeling that they won't be caught? Some people come across as inherently clueless, vulnerable, insecure and naïve. These are the type of people manipulators prey on. They believe a person who has low confidence, a low sense of self-worth or is clueless about the ways of the world is less likely to figure out that he/she is being manipulated.

Also, manipulators know that in the event that their manipulation cover is blown, the victim will not be able to do much. They cleverly pick targets who are low in confidence, self-acceptance, body image or sense of self-worth. It is easier to play on the vulnerabilities of these people than on assertive and self-assured people who won't allow people to take advantage of them.

For example, say a person has low awareness of social dynamics, doesn't understand jokes easily, doesn't identify a prank early, is unable to differentiate between genuine courtesy and sexual advances, can't tell when someone is genuinely attracted to them or simply wants to go to bed with them and other similar social and interpersonal dynamics. That person is more likely to be manipulated.

Manipulators are well aware that their victims can't do anything if they don't even realize that their weaknesses are being misused. They often cash in on the cluelessness of their victims by saying they are imagining things or making something up. An already clueless and unsure person is less likely to question this idea. When you are already reeling under feelings of insecurity, cluelessness and vulnerability, how difficult is it for a manipulator to take advantage of these feelings by reinforcing them further?

Manipulators

Manipulators manipulate because they think they can hurt or upset their victims more than the victims can hurt or upset them. They will almost always target people who come across as nice and vulnerable. When people are oblivious to the dishonesty existing within social relationships, they aren't really accustomed to dishonest allegiances. This doesn't equip them with the means to confront or counter dishonesty, which makes them less aware of being manipulated.

They Aren't Able to Accept Their Shortcomings

When people are unable to come to terms with their shortcomings or do not accept the responsibility or accountability for their faults, there is an inherent need to make others feel lesser than them.

If manipulators aren't good enough or feel miserable about themselves, there is a desire to make others feel equally worthless or miserable about themselves. When a person believes he/she is unworthy of someone, they will manipulate the person to feel unworthy, too. They can then gain control over his/her perception that they need the manipulator in their life to feel worthy. By putting others down or gaining control over others, they experience a form of pseudo superiority. If they can't be good enough for others, they make others feel like they aren't good enough to retain control over them.

In effect, manipulators don't want their victims to realize that they (the manipulators) aren't good enough or unworthy of them (the victims). The manipulator will therefore carefully cultivate a feeling of helplessness and unworthiness within the victim to keep them hooked to him/her. If a person realizes that he/she is more attractive, intelligent, richer, capable, efficient, self-sufficient etc., the higher their chances will be of leaving the manipulator. On the other hand, if the manipulator injects a feeling of the person not being 'complete,' they'll need someone to 'complete' them.

Manipulators are not able to accept their shortcomings or deal with criticism. They are often grappling with deep psychological issues or insecurities. By manipulating others, they do not have to confront their own insecurities to feel higher than others. For someone operating with such a narrow perspective, even a little correction, feedback or criticism can seem like a huge defeat.

People who manipulate don't know how to deal with defeat. When you hesitate to give feedback because the person will get defensive or blow things out of proportion or won't take things in the right spirit, it may be a sign you are dealing with someone who can't come to terms with criticism.

Notice how manipulators will seldom express feelings of gratitude or thankfulness. They find it challenging to be grateful to others because, in their view, by doing so they are increasing their sense of being obligated to another person, which doesn't give them an upper hand in any relationship.

For example, if you do someone a huge favor, they feel obliged to return that favor, which puts you above them in the relationship dynamics until they return the favor. Manipulators don't want to give you the upper hand by feeling obliged to you. Therefore, they will demonstrate minimal gratefulness, so you don't believe you've done something huge for them or that they are obliged to you. The idea is to always be one-up on you, and this feeling of being indebted to you doesn't make them feel one-up.

How To Analyze And Manipulate People

As explored, there are many stimuli that trigger human responses and lead to decision-making, and researchers have developed extensive methods to measure these outcomes, whether using biometrics, surveys, or focus groups. However, these research methods may not be at your disposal on a daily basis. Below are methods techniques you can use in everyday interactions to analyze cognitive and behavioral processes of individuals around you.

Observe Body Language

Research found that body language accounts for 55% of how we communicate, while words only account for 7%. The tone of voice represents the rest. People can tend to be over-analytical when reading human behavior and it may seem counterintuitive, but in order to be objective in analyzing people, observe naturally and try not to over-analyze.

Appearance

One of the first things that speak the loudest is the appearance of an individual. Take notice of a person's dressing. Is he or she dressed sharply in a suit, traditional clothing, or casual style? Does he or she look particularly conscious about the choice of clothing or hairstyle? The way a person dresses can determine his or her level of self-esteem.

Posture

When reading people's posture, observe if they hold their head high or slouch. Do they walk indecisively or walk with a confident chest? How do they esteem themselves? Posture also reveals confidence levels or a person's physical pain points.

Movements

People generally lean towards things they like, and away from things they do not. Crossed arms and legs suggest self-protection, anger, or defensiveness. When people cross their legs, their toes point to the person they are most comfortable with, or away from those they are not. When hands are placed in pockets, laps, or behind the back, it is an indication that the person is hiding something. Nervousness can also be revealed through lip-biting or cuticle-picking. Some people do that to soothe themselves under pressure or in awkward situations.

Facial Expressions

Aforementioned, emotions may not be visible unless expressed. Frown lines indicate over-thinking or worry, while crow's feet evidence joyfulness. Tension, anger, or bitterness can be seen on pursed lips or clenched jaws. Facial expressions can be one of the most evident ways to read human behavior towards specific things, places, or people.

How to analyze people effectively and efficiently

So, you want to learn how to analyze people effectively and efficiently. Well, you came to the right place! I will teach you everything you need to know about reading others. I will even teach you how to understand yourself. We need to talk about a few things before we get into the meat of the matter, however.

There are so many different methods to analyze others, and it can be hard to pick it all apart. Where did this practice come from? Why is it important to understand how to analyze others?

As it turns out, the art of analyzing others has existed

since–well, we had the intelligence to do it. Human beings are, by nature, herd animals. We are highly in tune with others, and our lives are driven by societal expectations. It can be easy to get caught up in our instincts, though, and to forget that we need to tackle things logistically. This is where learning how to actively analyze others comes in.

Studies consistently show that we are attracted to confidence and leadership. We like to take the burdens of everyday life and put them on other people's shoulders. Part of this is allowing ourselves to be far too trusting in situations where we would benefit from awareness surrounding red flags. Unfortunately, people are not always genuine; they can be terrible–evil, even. This is a world where we need to be on high alert. While analyzing people will help you in many aspects, such as work and in leadership roles, it can also help keep you safe.

Being situationally aware is simply not in practice anymore. People are constantly unaware of their surroundings and putting themselves in harm's way as a result.

So, as you can see, there are many reasons to unravel

the techniques of analyzation. Scanning people for warning signs or just for information about them puts you ahead of the pack. There is nothing more beneficial to your life, your relationships, and your protection. Spot narcissists before they have a chance to victimize you. Understand your boss's motives and learn how to nail down what they want from you, without even hearing them say it.

Here are some jobs which actively employ analyzing others:

- Politicians
- Lawyers
- Criminal investigators
- Military officials
- Psych professionals
- Forensic experts

As you can see, it truly is a universal tool. Many different people have to analyze others daily in their day-to-day lives.

I hope that these are the skills you want to learn. They

are invaluable, and it is my pleasure to help you improve your life, one impression at a time.

There are, of course, incredible benefits to consuming the knowledge I am offering to you today. First off, you will find that you can communicate your needs to other people far more effectively. Being able to tell how they are reacting and changing your approach accordingly is more than helpful. Communication is the most important skill that we can hone, quite frankly. It helps ease tension, earn the confidence of others, and put us in a positive light. Emotional intelligence goes hand in hand with communication as well.

This is another skill that will be furthered when paired with the power to analyze others. Your emotional intelligence greatly relies on your ability to understand others. The goal is always to meet people where they are: understanding what they need and being able to tell how they need to be handled. Whether you lead a team, need to help your children through their struggles, or are feeling the tension in your love life, I am here to help.

Strong relationships are the glue of society and, more importantly, of families. We need to know how to handle our spouses, children, and anybody else directly related to us. Strained relationships lead to strained relations, and none of us want to be caught up in a family feud. Learning how people tick and how to handle tough situations is the key. You will also learn how to watch for red flags with your children. Knowing how to read their body language and pick up on their verbal cues do wonders for seeing warning signs well in advance.

If you are a parent, this will be a key book in taking your parenting to the following level.

As for another skill, leadership, you will soon be at the front of the crowd. You will find that people not only listen to you but that they actively want to listen to you. Becoming a strong leader means being able to tell who a person is just by carefully observing them. True leaders understand the absolute power that body language holds. After all, it is the oldest form of communication of them all.

Many leaders in the business world, as well as in other areas, actively take lessons and classes on analyzing others. This is a skill which can be applied in almost every situation you can think of. It builds your confidence knowing that when you take the lead, others follow suit.

I am pretty sure you are beginning to get the idea of

what analyzing others can do for you. The benefits are boundless, and there are new ones at every corner. You cannot imagine how much life will change!

I would like to get you started with a few rules. As you can imagine, there is a baseline to start when it comes to analyzing others. You can remember some steps to help you begin which are not hard and fast but excellent for helping you to understand the process. Practice makes perfect, so make sure you pay close attention to this list.

These rules are as follows:

1.   Understand What Their Baseline Is: Everybody is just a tad bit different from the rest. It is almost like how parents can tell their twins apart, but nobody else can. Learning how to analyze others means you can tell them apart on a much different level. Understand that you can only tell their "baseline" after knowing them for a while.

You can watch for signs that they are nervous. Perhaps ask probing questions you know will elicit the emotion you want to pin down. If they tend to become physical restless under duress, you know what sort of body language to watch for.

This is the first rule for many reasons. Most importantly, it reminds us that we need to see the whole person. Cold reading is great.

2.   Notice the Changes: Take into account the entire picture of the person. This builds off of the first rule. Understand that any gesture can mean something, but you need to put several clues together to really solve the mystery that is a person.

This will also build off of noticing what signs of nervousness you may be looking for. We are using nervousness for these examples, but it goes for any emotion. Anger, unease, discomfort–they are all negative emotions you can begin to pinpoint.

3.   Watch For Warning Signs. When certain behaviors are brought into the light and therefore meaning in your eyes, you can start to piece it together. If you have noticed that they shift their eyes around when nervous, and their eyes tighten up when they are angry, you will know when you are treading on dangerous territory.

There are several different clusters of behaviors that can be seen across the board. As mentioned, humans are pack animals in nature. This means that we have learned how to communicate with each other whether we like it or not. Certain tip-offs are pretty well-known. However, a lot more will be missed to the untrained eye. That is why you are reading this!

4. 	Compare Behavior Changes: The following rule in this line-up is to always make sure you watch how they behave with others as well. It is a popular belief that you do not watch the person who is speaking–you watch the reaction of the person you want to impress. Making sure you are taking note of your boss's body language while listening to co-workers, for example.

Notice the changes between them talking to you and them talking to others. This will help cue you into their true emotions about you as well as how they feel about others. Are their arms crossing when they talk to their friends? Is their body still turned towards you even while engaged in conversation elsewhere?

5. 	Watch Yourself. One of the most powerful things you can do is be aware of your body language. We do not just need to understand others but also ourselves. We influence others with our facial expressions without even knowing what it looks like. That

is not what you want to be doing. To control a situation or a conversation, or even influence it, you need to practice expressions.

The best way to do this is to do it in the mirror.

6.   Listen To Others Talk. Identify the strongest person in the room. You will notice them right away, most likely. Sometimes, however, it takes a little time. Look for open body language being used purposefully but elegantly. A big smile, a voice that commands attention and self-confidence are all ways of saying "I am the boss in this situation." They do not need the approval of others and they often hold the most sway in the situation.

Same idea as watching the boss when others are talking. Even if somebody is technically the boss, that does not mean they are completely in control. A confident, strong person will make an impression and quickly become somebody whose opinion the "head honcho" deeply trusts. Knowing which strings to pull will push you further and further toward getting what you want out of a situation.

7.   Watch Them Move. Looking at body language while they talk to you, especially sitting or

standing still, is one thing. You also need to watch their general state of being while moving around. You can tell quite a bit about a person just by the way they walk and how they move. Confident people tend to stand tall, with their shoulders back and chest pushed a little out. They walk with purpose, as though they always have somewhere important to be.

On the other hand, somebody who is unsure of themselves embodies the exact opposite traits. They try to make themselves look small, perhaps hunching over a little, keeping their head low.

8.   Listen For Speech Patterns. Another rule is to listen closely to how they talk and what they are saying, both about the topic at hand and about themselves. How a person speaks tells you so much about them, both literally and figuratively! When you can identify how they speak when they are being truthful and genuine, you can figure out when they are being the opposite.

There are several different ways to go about this. However, looking for "action words" is one of the best. A lot of ex-agents talk about how looking for these words, especially strong verbs; it helps you figure out how their brain works. These words do not just convey their thoughts but they convey the patterns of their thoughts as well.

9.   Key Into Their Personality. The last rule is to always put all of this information together. You cannot use one of these rules without following up with the others. These are the cardinal tenets off of which all analyzation of others is built. Once you put together their verbal communication, their body language, and understand them as a whole, you have won half the battle.

It is especially important in the art of analyzing people that you follow this rule. Humans are, by nature, endlessly complex. We cannot be understood by just one piece of information or even a few pieces. Think of it like putting together a puzzle. In the beginning, you have no idea what the result will be. Once you begin to put some of the pieces together, you begin to understand the whole picture. You can even fill in some of the missing pictures once you have enough of those pieces.

So, as you can see, you eventually will build your skillset until you can fill in more information with only some of the pieces. But you still need those pieces.

These rules should be followed at all times. Keep them in mind whenever you go about trying to figure anybody out. They are key in your journey through the art of analyzation!

It can be easy to misunderstand which is which, especially when dealing with potentially dangerous situations. However, mixing them up due to inexperience or simply not knowing the difference can be far more troublesome. Paranoia at its most extreme form is a symptom of many mental illnesses. None of us are immune to falling into the trap of poor thought patterns which encourage paranoia to take hold. It is a sinister feeling that we all need to keep at bay.

Intuition is rooted almost solely in logic. It is the idea that you have cultivated an array of experiences in your life that you can compare to the situation at hand. It is a result of insight as well as the ability to properly analyze others. You will feel calm, stable, and rational when your intuition is kicking in. It does not feel like it is "forced" upon you in the same way that fear does. You have control over intuition and can reason your way through even the negative thoughts that come your way.

You can ascribe the following words to intuition:

- Collected

- In control

- Gentle

- Freeing

- Enlightening

As you can see, intuition is a highly positive emotion you should nurture. Always listen to that inner voice which nudges you towards good ideas. With a little bit of attention, you can quickly decide whether it is intuition you are feeling or simply anxiety and fear.

Speaking of which, let us talk a little bit about fear now. This is a strong emotion that overwhelms you. Fear eats away and pushes you towards rash behavior. You know fear well—we all do. This is an emotion we have all felt, probably many times over our lifespans. You cannot count how many times it has crept into your brain. It is not just an emotion, however.

It is something far more powerful. Fear can actively change the way you think and your ability to respond to situations. The part of the brain which controls it, the amygdala, shows signs of hyperactivity when you feel fear, and your frontal lobe's activity is stunted. These two regions are responsible for your reactions, your impulses, and your behavior.

Those are not the parts of yourself that you want to fall short on!

If it is fear you are feeling, the following words may suit it:

- Apprehensive

- Impulsive

- Irrational

- Cagey

- Insecure

Once you begin to tell the difference, you begin to take control back. Managing your negative emotions properly is one of the best steps in building your self-control. It also allows you to stay focused on situations even if they feel dangerous in any way.

Techniques Of Dark Psychology And Dark Manipulation

When it comes to the idea of influencing people, there are several techniques in dark psychology that are often used for this purpose. Typically, people use techniques of mind control to influence others. These techniques have been known to humans for several years.

Most people are fascinated by the thought of the possibility of someone being able to control their minds. Basically, this fascination is laced by fears of the possibilities of another person influencing them by being able to control their minds and get them to do things against their will.

There are a lot of conspiracy theories about the way governments and those in positions of power influence people by controlling their minds and getting them to do things against their will. As a matter of fact, there have been court cases where defendants claim that they committed the crimes they are being accused of as a result of the influence of brainwashing.

Regardless of the fact that many people talk about the influence of mind control, very little is yet known by most people about the different techniques of dark psychology that can be used to influence people through mind control, and the mode of operation of each of these techniques.

Though there are many ways of influencing people, the techniques of mind control are the most common, and they are brainwashing, persuasion, hypnosis, manipulation, and deception.

Brainwashing

Brainwashing is simply a way of convincing people to let go of those things that they hitherto believed in so that they can pick up new values and ethics. There are several ways in which this type of influence is exerted, though not all of them fall under dark psychology.

Take a person who has traveled to live in a different country, for example. Chances are the person who is going to be influenced by certain factors of change as a result of his new environment so that the person can easily fit into and function in his new society.

Dark psychology, on the other hand, is manifested when a dictator takes over power and tries to brainwash his/her subjects to accept his dictates in order to rule peacefully. This type of influence also manifests in concentration camps.

There are, however, a lot of misconceptions about the topic of brainwashing. When it comes to exerting this kind of influence, some people have some perverted ideas about the practice, and this includes techniques used by governments to influence their subjects, which they seem to manipulate like a remote control.

Also, there are people who do not seem to believe in the efficacy of brainwashing, so they think people are lying when they claim to have been brainwashed.

When people are being brainwashed, they will be convinced to change their viewpoint on a particular subject by making use of different strategies to influence the way they think and see things. During this process, people do not merely rely on a single strategy, and for this reason, one cannot easily capture the practice into a single idea or thought.

Typically, the targets of brainwashing get isolated from the things they are familiar with, and their emotions will become broken such that they become vulnerable. It is in this state of emotional vulnerability that new concepts are introduced to them. As the subjects assimilate this concept, the brainwasher rewards them for putting the thoughts into practice or for expressing the thoughts in line with the new ideas.

The reward for putting the new ideas into practice is used for reinforcement for the brainwashing that is taking its course.

Persuasion

This is another technique used in influencing people, and it is closely related to manipulation. The aim of this technique is to influence the character, intentions, attitudes, and beliefs or values of the target. This technique is used everyday dealings with people and institutions.

Sometimes, this influencing technique is an important aspect of communication, which helps to get people of different mindsets to consolidate and agree on a particular subject matter. This technique is used in business to get people to change their mindset about a product, idea, or event that is taking place. To do this, written or spoken words are used to pass thoughts, ideas, feelings, or messages to others.

Persuasion is also used for selfish reasons in order to

achieve personal goals. It is commonly used during trials, by sales representatives to give sales pitches and by politicians during electioneering campaigns. Though these reasons may not be considered as bad or evil reasons, they remain dark psychology techniques that are used to get the subject to act or think in a way that is contrary to their original line of thought or reasoning.

Some scholars define persuasion as a technique that makes use of an individual's powers or resources to alter the behavior or attitudes of other people. It is important to note that there are different types of persuasion which are as follows:

Systemic Persuasion: This involves the process of making use of logic and appeals to change and influence other people's ways of life or reasoning.

Heuristic Persuasion: This is the type of persuasion that involves changing a person's attitudes and beliefs by appealing to the person's emotions or habits.

Persuasion, as an agent of dark influence, is always used in every society. Take, for instance, when you are talking to a person about some political or religious ideologies, you are going to try to persuade them to start thinking the way you think. Also, during political campaigns, every politician tries to persuade their listeners to vote for them. A sales representative who is trying to sell a new product to a client tries everything within his/her power to influence the client's decision by trying to persuade him to buy the product he is selling.

Persuasion as a form of influence is so common that people do not even realize that they are being influenced by it at all. The only time it becomes a problem is in cases when a person devotes all of his time to persuade a person to adopt ideals or sets of beliefs that are not in line with his/her own values.

Manipulation

Manipulation is another dark technique that is used in influencing people. There are many ways of using this technique to influence the thought pattern of the target.

To achieve their aim, manipulators use insults, deceits, and other underhanded strategies, and they do their bidding without considering the welfare or the emotions of their targets.

This is a very potent method of dark psychology as it makes use of cunning, abusive, and exploitative methods. Most times, people are able to realize that they are being manipulated, and people are also able to point out the fact that someone close to them is being manipulated, but they do not always regard it as a technique of dark psychology.

Deception

This is also a way of influencing people using dark psychology as a way of controlling the minds of others. Here, the subjects are made to sell ideas, events, or things which are not true or which never happened. These ideas that the agent tries to sell absolute lies or twisted versions of the truth.

Deception also has to do with other things like propaganda, dissimulation, secrecy, disguise, and distraction. This is also a dangerous dark technique as the subject does not also know that dark psychology. They may not easily find out because they have been presented with a lie and made to believe that it's the truth. It gets more difficult when the truth that is being hidden from the subject is something that could keep them away from harm's way.

Manipulation Techniques

As you may already know, manipulators make use of everything within his power to work so hard to reach his goals and satisfy his selfish needs. To reach these goals, a person who wishes to manipulate another makes use of several techniques to influence people to do the things they want them to do. Five of the most common techniques that are used by manipulators are blackmail, emotional blackmail, debasing others, telling lies, and creating illusions.

Blackmail

This is usually a manipulator's first strategy in trying to influence a target. It is said to be actions that involve threatening someone else. These threats are often not justified, but they are aimed at getting something out of the target or cause them to lose something if they do not do the bidding of the manipulator.

Blackmail can also be said to be a way of coercing someone else by threating them. The agents, in this case, tell the target that they are going to face criminal prosecution and threaten them that they are going to take their money. They may even be threatened with physical harm.

Emotional Blackmail

This is also another strategy that is used by manipulators to get their subjects to do their bidding. In using this technique, the manipulator induces a feeling of guilt or sympathy in their targets. These emotions are very strong feelings that humans experience, and they are capable of making people act according to the will of the manipulator.

Once these feelings have been induced in the subject, the manipulator takes advantage of the feeling to get what they really want from the subject. With this, it is easy for them to coerce the target to do what they want or help them in a way that they ordinarily wouldn't.

Debasing Others

In order to get others to help them to achieve their goals, another technique that manipulators use is to debase others in order to get them to help them to achieve their goals. This is a technique that has proven to be very easy as the manipulator simply tries to lower the self-esteem of his/her target.

In most cases, the manipulator does not try to verbally debase his subjects because they are going to feel like the manipulator is trying to attach his person, and this will make them raise their guard. In this case, the target will no longer be willing to help the manipulator achieve his or her goals. Hence they begin to keep as much distance as they can from the manipulator, and this will make it hard for them to reach their final goals.

Lying

Regardless of what the aim of the manipulator is, one thing they are always very good at is telling lies, and they are always going to do this till they are able to achieve their goals fully. In order to reach their ultimate goal, there are several types of lies that manipulators tell. They either tell complete lies or leave out some parts of the truth about certain topics.

One of the main reasons why manipulators tell lies is because they are well aware of the fact that the truth is not going to help them to achieve their goals as much as their lies would. Most times, they feel like people may not want to help them if they tell the truth. This means that the truth is going to

ruin their chances of succeeding in what they want completely.

Creating Illusions

This is a technique that the manipulator combines with lying in order to excellently achieve their final goals, regardless of whose ox is gored. They create illusions by creating an image of their choice and then make their target feel like this image, which is an illusion is the reality. It does not matter to the manipulator that the image he has created is not real.

In order to achieve their aims, manipulators go as far as creating shreds of evidence that they need to drive their point home to the point they are trying to prove, in line with their selfish goals.

In creating their illusion, manipulators create ideas in their targets' minds and back the ideas up with evidence. Once they have been able to create these ideas, the manipulators withdraw for some days and watch the effect of their manipulation take its full course in the minds of their targets for some time.

Controlling Others with Confusion and Compulsion

Typically, in dealing with humans, there is always a level of conscious manipulation, coercion, and influence that takes place, but when a relationship is healthy, those involved will be able to strike a balance with time and consistency.

In cases where a person is dealing with another person who has high tendencies of manipulating others, the manipulator has all the power, and he wields this power by confusing and using compulsion on the other person, and they sometimes make the victim feel like they are the ones that are actually in charge.

When a person who is prone to manipulation gets into a relationship with a person who is very manipulative, it is often very dangerous because the manipulator is going to use compulsion on the subject a lot, and he/she is also going to get confused a lot.

Below are some of the ways which manipulators use compulsion and confusion on their targets:

The Manipulator Opens A Trap

Using control and compulsion on a target is not quite different from any other type of manipulation technique. This is much easier when a target is a person that acts in a particular way that they want to harness, and they simply create some positive strokes as often as possible.

Once these strokes are created, one may not see any visible difference as all the parties involved in the relationship are largely at peace with each other at this stage. Everything is normal, and they don't have any issues doing things for the sake of one another. In rare cases, the contrary may be the case, but it only means that things may have started off badly.

The Manipulator Places Bait in The Trap

When the manipulator has successfully confused the target, he then proceeds to place bait on the trap he has set. This may be a direct trap or a camouflaged trap that comes in the form of an offer of a very juicy reward. In work environments, the target may be promised a promotion or a pay rise. In an intimate relationship, the bait may be a sex offer or a promise of a blissful life together forever in marriage.

There are men and women who have become accustomed to the fluctuating nature of their partners who may want them today and not want them tomorrow. Some women have been roped in with the promise of marriage as bait, but never get proposed to even after several years. The reverse may also be the case.

Creating Compulsive Behavior

By setting a trap and placing a bait on the trap, the manipulator is able to cage the subject into their strings, and because the effects of the manipulation is getting the best of them, as well as the stress and uncertainty that comes with it, the victim is usually unable to withdraw a bit to see a clear picture of the things that are really happening and the effects they are having on them.

People that are seeing things from outside, who are not involved in the manipulative relationship are able to notice the way the subject acts whenever they are around the manipulator as opposed to the way they act when they are in the presence of other people, though there is never a clear indicator for the difference in attitude.

In some cases, the manipulator is also able to alter their behavior such that they decide how their subjects act in the presence of other people. This way, their relationship looks healthy before others. Though the victim may seem happier when they are with others, they may not be able to figure out why it is so.

Often times, the manipulators are able to figure out the emotions of their subjects without much struggle. When they seem to be happy for too long, they find ways to bring it down by dampening their spirit.

At this stage, the victim is already used to the intermittent threats and rewards, and he becomes conditioned to act accordingly. These threats or rewards do not necessarily need to have any connection with the behavior of the victim, and this type of treatment creates a compulsive behavior in the victim.

Whenever rewards are linked to the actions of a person, the person's actions stop whenever the rewards are no longer available. When on the other hand, the rewards of action change slowly and inconsistently, people find themselves going on for a long time after they have received the first reward, with hopes of receiving another.

How To Talk

THE POWER OF PERSUASION

The power of persuasion means nothing more than using mental abilities to form words and feelings used to convince other people to do things they may or may not want to do. Some people are better able to persuade than other people. And some people are easier to persuade then other people.

The ease of persuading other people is directly tied to their current mental or emotional state. Someone who is lonely or tired is easier to persuade, simply because their defenses are lowered. Someone who is momentarily needy may be easier to persuade than someone who has a strong sense of self-worth. People who are at a low point in their lives are easy prey for others who might try to persuade them to do something they might not usually do.

Think of the publicity surrounding religious cults in the past. Everyone wanted to know how someone could fall prey to the teachings and ideals of the cult. The answer is simple: the victim was seeking something the cult offered. Whether the dangling carrot was food and shelter or love or religious freedom, the cult offers something tangible to the person who feels their life is lacking something important. And the person who joins the cult does not see themselves as a victim, but a participant. Think back further to the flower children of the sixties and seventies. These people lived in communes where everyone had a particular role to play. Some people would grow gardens to feed the members of the commune while others might wash laundry or clean houses. Everyone helped everyone else. The idea behind living in a commune was to leave behind the trappings that 'society' deemed as markers of success, such as fat paychecks and huge houses. These people wanted to live simply and enjoy what love and Mother Nature had to offer.

For every good group that assembles for the good of the people and works to help its members, there are countless groups that are brought together by forces that have no desire other than controlling other people for their own good. These leaders are very charismatic and very dangerous, because a person who is temporarily weak in mind or in the soul may not be able to resist their promises. It is important for everyone to understand how persuasion works in order to be able to resist it when needed.

The first step in persuasion involves the idea of reciprocating. If a person does something nice for someone else, then the receiving person usually feels the need to do something good in return. If someone helps their elderly neighbor carry in groceries from the car, that neighbor might feel obligated to bake homemade cookies for that person. A coworker who helps complete a project is more likely to receive assistance when it is needed. Many people do nice things for others all the time without expecting anything in return. The person who does nice things for people and then mentions some little favor that can be done in return may be someone to watch closely.

Nonprofit organizations use this tactic to gain more contributions to their causes. They will often send some little trinket or gift to prompt people to donate larger sums of money, or even just to donate where they might not have originally. The idea behind this is that the person opening the letter has received a little gift for no reason, so they might feel obligated to give something in return.

The consistency of self is the following step. People who

commit to something, through verbal or written methods, are more likely to follow through on the idea that someone who makes no promises, Even if the original motivation is gone or the original incentive was taken away, people see this promise as being part of their image. They made a promise. This is often why counselors tell people to write their goals down. People are more likely to follow a written list they can refer to daily.

It is easy enough to change someone's image of themselves, especially if that person is needy or mentally weak. During times of war, it is customary to get prisoners to denounce their own country in order to hopefully turn others against that country. This is easy enough to do when starved prisoners are also mentally weak and have few defenses to use to deflect their captors. By constantly repeating statements that denounce the home country the captive begins to believe what they are saying because it must be true because they are saying it.

Another thing to be careful of is what is known as the herd mentality. Humans live in groups. Most of us want to belong to the herd and want to enjoy the safety being in a herd brings. Monkey see, monkey do. People tend to mirror the behavior seen around them. Think of the story of the emperor that runs around with no clothes on. His tailors had him convinced he was wearing fine garments, so he convinced all the people of his kingdom. And because they could not question the king, they had to believe what he was saying. This can also work in seriously negative ways. Think of the mob mentality. This is just another way to follow the herd, but it usually involves illegal or dangerous activities engaged in only because someone else was doing the same thing.

Some people are automatically tempted to follow authority. People in positions of authority can command blind respect to their authority simply by acting a certain way or putting on a uniform. The problem with this is that authority figures or those that look like authority figures, can cause some people to do extraordinary things they would not normally do had a person in a position of authority not been the one asking. And it is not simply held to people in uniform. People who carry themselves a certain way or speak a certain way can give the impression that they are something they are not.

For someone or something to be considered a credible authority, it must be familiar and people must have trust in the person or organization. Someone who knows all there is to know about a subject is considered an expert and is more likely to be trusted than someone who has limited knowledge of the subject. But the information must also make sense to the people hearing it. If there is not some semblance of accuracy and intelligence then the authority figure loses credibility. Even the person who is acknowledged as an expert will lack persuasive abilities if they are seen as not being trustworthy.

People want to be liked. People want to like other people. The problem is when some people use this fact to cause other people to do things they might not ordinarily do. People who are easy to like usually come across as very persuasive. People want to believe them. Con artists are extremely likeable people. The problem is that even likeable people may not have your personal best interests at heart. In fact, they probably only have their own interest in mind. Even someone who is totally legitimate, like a salesperson, is really most interested in their own interests. They may want their customer to be perfectly happy with their purchase so they will recommend that salesperson to their friends, but their ultimate concern is with themselves and their sales goals.

The worst part of the power that goes along with persuasion is that things that are scarce or hard to get are seen as much more valuable. People value diamonds because they are expensive and beautiful. If they were merely pretty stones, they would not be as interesting. Inconsistent rewards are a lot more interesting than consistent rewards. If a cookie falls every time a person rings a bell, then they are less likely to spend a lot of time ringing the bell because they know the cookie reward will always appear. If, however, the cookie only appears sometimes, people will spend much more time ringing the bell just in case this is the time the cookie will fall.

There are ways to improve the power of persuasion. Just like any other trait, it can be made stronger by following a few strategies and by regular practice.

Never hesitate to ask others what they think. Usually, those in a position of authority will not look for advice from other people. This is an opportunity many leaders neglect to take advantage of. Instead of asking others for their opinion and ideas, they miss the chance to make everyone feel like part of the group with an equal role to play. Besides, leaders who are not afraid to ask for input from others might learn something they did not know before.

Always remember to ask for advice, not feedback. People love being asked to give advice. Asking for feedback means that an opinion has already been given and the speaker wants to know what everyone else thinks of their own opinion. In many situations, there will be no responses because no one wants to disagree or be seen as argumentative, particularly with an authority figure. But asking for advice gives people a chance to voice their own opinions.

Before asking for any type of assistance, set the stage. People do not like being put on the spot. Walking up to someone and immediately asking for a favor sends two messages. The first one is that the favor is more important than the person. In this case, the favor needed is the focus of the conversation. Say that Bob walks into the room, goes straight up to Bill and asks Bill to assist at a fundraiser that weekend. Bill is caught off guard and must make an immediate decision. Does he say no, in front of others, and look like a mean-spirited person for not helping at the fundraiser? Or does he answer with yes without really knowing if he wants to do it or not?

Now if Bob had bothered to set the stage for asking for the favor, he would have approached the conversation in a totally different manner. First, he would have approached Bill with a friendly greeting and cheerful smile. He would take a few minutes to make small talk with Bill, perhaps asking about his work life or his family life. After chatting cheerfully for a few minutes Bob would approach the idea of the fundraiser in a casual manner. "Hey, Bill, by the way…." He would explain what he needed Bill to do, explain how much he would really enjoy having Bill's presence at the fundraiser, then asking Bill to get back with him as soon as possible with an answer. He would assure Bill that whatever decision he made would be fine, although he really hoped Bill would be able to join him.

What is the difference between the two situations? In the second situation, Bill feels wanted. He feels needed. He feels as though his presence, or the lack of it, is important to Bob. In the second situation, Bob is most likely to get an honest answer. And what if Bill is not able to help Bob at the fundraiser? Bill will be more likely to help Bob in the future because he not only feels valued but he feels like he owes Bob something, Bill would probably be thinking that he owed Bob one in the future.

Persuasion is a powerful tool in the game of life. Persuasive people know that they have an amazing power, and they know how to use it correctly. They know how to listen and really hear what other people have to say. They are very good at making a connection with other people, and this makes them seem even more honest and friendly. They make others feel that they are knowledgeable and can offer a certain sense of satisfaction. They also know when to momentarily retreat and regroup. They are not pushy. They are persuasive.

Conversational Skills Techniques

When people don't answer you, when they use sarcasm, telling you it's impossible to talk to you, threatening you with ultimatums, or talking to you like you were a child, these signs of psychological manipulation through language and communication are exhausting. This is a form of emotional abuse and mental exploitation that we must learn to recognize.

One of the most sinister men in Italian history was Licio Gelli. He was an agent of the Masonic Lodge Propaganda Due. He was a neo-fascist who specialized in manipulating masses. This evil person once said that to control anyone, you had to know how to communicate. He showed us that language can be used as a weapon and can be used to dominate.

Many people know this too well. Within the realm of politics, in media, in advertising there is constant use of manipulation to control us, influence our decisions, and yes, to seduce us. Once we come into our private realm, everything gets a bit more complex and mantic.

We are talking about the way we communicate with our friends, significant other, family, etc. If you just stop and look, you can see signs of emotional and psychological manipulation all around you, but these are usually camouflaged. You might also fall into a trap of using it yourselves. You must know how to detect it and how to react to it.

You must know that it isn't just important to watch what you say but how you say it.

Signs of Psychological Manipulation

When we talk about psychological manipulation by using words, what happens first will be an imbalance in a relationship. It is using language to benefit yourself. Not to just control a person but to harm them as well. Bare emotions are what cause this aggression in you.

Aldous Huxley once said that words are like X-rays. If they are used in a Machiavellian way, they could pierce through everything: another person's self-esteem, their identity, and dignity. You must learn to see them coming, to know a bit more about this personally. Here are some warning signs:

Manipulating facts

Anyone who is an expert in manipulating through communication is a strategist who is great at twisting the truth. They will always turn everything around to their favor, lower their share of responsibility, and blame anyone but themselves. They will also withhold and exaggerate important information to make sure the balance will always tilt toward their "truth."

They say you are impossible to talk to

This approach is effective, direct, and very simple. If anyone tells you that "you are impossible to talk to," they are avoiding exactly what you are wanting to do: talking about the problem. It's common for them to say you are too emotional, you are "making a mountain out of a molehill," and they can't talk with you. They will accuse you of what they have problems with, and this is poor communication skills.

Harassing intellectually

An emotional and psychological manipulator uses another common strategy: intellectual harassment. They will constantly throw arguments your way. They will also make sure the information is different and the facts are so twisted just trying to emotionally exhaust you and convince you that they are correct.

Ultimatums with no time to decide

You might have heard someone say: "If you can't accept what I am saying, then it's all over." They might have gone one further with you have until tomorrow to think about it. This communication style is very distressing and painful. They have put you between a rock and a hard place and generate a lot of emotional suffering along with anxiety.

You must know that is somebody respects you, and truly loves you, they will never use "all or nothing" threats. This is just one more manipulation strategy.

Constantly saying your name while talking

If somebody constantly says your name during a heated conversation, they are using a control mechanism. When they do this, they are forcing you to pay attention and causing you to feel intimidated.

Black humor and irony

If they like using black humor and irony, they are trying to ridicule and humiliate you. This is another sign of psychological manipulation in communication. They are trying to belittle you and trying to impose their superiority on you.

Using evasiveness or silence

If they say things like: "Now isn't a good time", "I don't want to talk about it", "Why are you bringing that up now?" All of this is common with significant others, especially if one doesn't have a good sense of responsibility or communication skills.

Claiming ignorance

If somebody says to you: "I don't understand what you mean," this is another tactic. They will pretend not to understand what you are wanting them to do or say. They are playing mind games. They want to make it look like you are complicating things and the conversation doesn't make any sense. This is a strategy that passive-aggressive manipulators like to use to avoid taking responsibility and wants to make you suffer.

They allow you to talk first

The most subtle sign of psychological manipulation is when they always make you talk first. By doing this, they achieve many things. The first one is buying time to get their argument ready. The second is to figure out your weak points. It is common that after they have listened to you, they won't express their opinion or ideas. They will only ask more questions. Rather than reaching some sort of an agreement, they try to highlight your shortcomings. They will direct the conversation in ways that make you look weak and clumsy.

Yes, there are many other strategies that emotional and psychological manipulator could use when communicating but the above are the most common. These try to intimidate you and keep you from establishing effective dialogues, but they try to subdue you. They are trying to incapacitate you on all levels: mentally, emotionally, and personally. You must learn how to see these destructive strategies.

Silent Treatment = Emotional Abuse

what does "silent treatment" mean? It is refusing to verbally engage with another person, often because of a conflict within the relationship. Some refer to it as stonewalling or the cold shoulder. It is used as a passive-aggressive way to control others. It can be considered emotional abuse. If you think it is normal for your significant other to go for days without speaking to you, think again. Silence can be used productively like right after a breakup or if you are taking a time to cool off but prolonged times of unresponsiveness in relationships aren't healthy or normal.

At times, you might not have anything to say. Sometimes disconnecting is a good idea so that each party can take a moment to reflect on what has happened and then come back once they have received some clarity. Arguments aren't ever pleasant, but they come and go and might leave new understanding.

Most of us have been at a place where we don't want to face the argument and it is not because we fear an escalation. We refuse to go back in because we are trying to punish them.

The silent treatment is one of the most powerful tools that a passive-aggressive manipulator could use. It keeps their opponent on edge while giving you a sense of power. It demands emotional and mental perfection from other people that don't exist in anyone. Ignoring somebody like this is very hurtful. All the emotional effects might last and frankly, this is very unfair.

Dealing with It

If you are the one that is being ignored and you want to work through it, what can you do about it?

Apologize? Grovel? They are useless because the goal of the silent treatment is to make you suffer. You don't want yourself to suffer. You also don't want your loved one to feel like they must trap you into suffering in order to have control over you.

In order to react to this treatment requires a dose of humility, understanding, openness, and sensitivity. What you can do is simple, and you don't have to "take the high road" in the situation. Stances like this are just variations of you falling right into the trap they set because you will soon get tired of trying to fix things.

What you can do is be honest, since this is what you want from them, right? You can say something like: "I would really love to figure out what is wrong," since it requires two people to have an argument.

You must be sincere, and you shouldn't pretend that you haven't noticed their silent treatment; that is simply putting gas on a fire. Acting honestly won't be easy because you will be confused. You feel hurt and guilty, which is a dangerous mix. Creating this mixture of feelings is what the manipulator wants. They want you to be voiceless and feel horrible, which makes you feel terrible.

When you are faced with the silent treatment, it's like trying to play a game of Clue with the board flipped over and without any pieces. You want to be able to solve the problem, but this has more to do with not knowing what you have done wrong or something so tiny the silencer feels the need to control the relationship for some time.

Being the receiver of this manipulation is extremely hard. Not understanding what was done, not understanding what you should say, your feelings being disrespected and disregarded, all the doubts that are planted on if the relationship was viable, as well as the guilt of feeling you created a crack in something wonderful, is a game you will eventually lose. It doesn't do anything but drop more anger onto a volatile situation.

Getting out of this type of situation will take a lot of patience. This is what is needed if you want to continue the relationship. The silencer's cycle of allowing you to come back is just a blame game that they have thought up for you to overlook any damage that they have caused.

Simplicity

Feeling like you have fed your significant other poison and you are struggling to find a way to fix it is no way to

113

live. Don't accept anyone's ploy for power, never internalize it, and don't accept it as being a sign that you are a failure. Understand this, you didn't do anything wrong. Having a grievance is one thing, but constantly being treated unfairly from others isn't.

If you are emotionally abusive, overbearing, or manipulative, too, there isn't anything you should do but say goodbye to each other. The silent treatment's main purpose is to wear you down. Granted, we have heard all sorts of advice from others about love. Communication and love aren't a game of picking sides, keeping score, or winning.

There are two rules that will serve us well during our time here: "Being good to each other and being good for each other." This type of situation isn't an either, or. This is an "and" situation and you must make sure it stays that way, or you will spin out of control.

Using the silent treatment isn't a good way to satisfy these things. And no matter what anybody else has to say, the single word, Hi, can provide you with satisfaction. This hi may be awkward, and it could make you feel like you are drowning or like a restrained panther, but it must be said.

Reality is a great place to start a conversation. But silence can sometimes sound like a scream

When is Silent Treatment Right?

There is a place and time for silence. There are circumstances where silence is recommended. In toxic relationships where one person tries to resolve the conflict, but the aggression is escalated silence is acceptable. Staying quiet is a way to help you cope with the person and situation. Silence can be used to protect and to help calm down after an altercation.

Silence can also be used as a boundary if you have just removed yourself from a relationship with a sociopath or narcissist.

How to Know if Silence is Abusive

You must ask yourself: "Am I being forced to defend myself or am I the one attacking them?" This is where you will find the difference. If you remain silent just to gain an upper hand and to make them suffer, then that is abuse.

If you keep your mouth shut to avoid suffering abuse, that is self-defense. If you aren't sure, it will help to answer these following few questions:

You are calm again, but you still expect them to make the following move.

When an argument happens, it might take time for feelings to come back down. Silence in these situations isn't bad since it can keep you doing or saying something you might regret.

If you are staying silent, act after you have calmed down since you will insist that they make the first move toward reconciliation. This is a bit abusive. If you want to talk, open a dialogue.

Will just a complete apology do?

Will you stay silent for as long as they don't give you an apology? They might have shown some remorse and are trying to make amends. It isn't what you had in mind while you are ruminating. If efforts have been made toward an apology, it is right for you to move from your position to end the treatment you have given them.

This isn't saying that you have forgiven them, but you should have a conversation about what happened and why it makes you feel like you do. When you don't engage, you are choosing to keep them back which might be emotional abuse.

Are you responsible for the disagreement?

At times the other person is completely wrong. There are things that aren't excusable. This isn't always the case. If you are keeping silent despite fault falling at your feet, you are ignoring the role you had in the argument that led you to where you are. This is abusive because it puts all the blame on the other person and makes them feel bad.

Will you keep this up for a certain time frame?

When somebody does something that annoys you, don't think that you aren't going to talk with them for the remainder of the day. This can be viewed as abusive since it is giving a sentence for the crime, no matter how you may feel at any time in the future. It is telling the other person they deserve this punishment. It doesn't leave any room for forgiveness or feelings getting better between the two of you.

Secrets of Persuasive People, How to Stop And Spot Manipulation

Manipulation is about control and gain. They need to control a person and the situation in order to get whatever it is they are after. While each set of circumstances are different, there are still some very common tactics that manipulators use, think of them as a general blueprint. They can be altered a bit based on certain situations, but they are all generally the same. The ways in which people can be manipulated are also different; for instance, the way someone manipulates someone in a romantic relationship is not going to be same in friendship and so on. The good news is that the basic principles are similar enough that if you learn to spot one manipulative situation, it can make it easier to spot more in the future.

No matter what type of situation, manipulators still have similar tactics that they will use simply because they work. They will change them a bit depending on their specific wants and the situation at hand, but manipulative behavior is not the norm so it can still be spotted if you know what you're looking for. Even if they think they are breaking the mold, a manipulator is doing what countless manipulators have done before them. This doesn't make their behavior any better or acceptable, but it does make them somewhat predictable. If you are the victim of manipulation, you might be able to see it for what it is, but others do, and this is important because when you want to cut a manipulator out of your life, those are the people you can depend on.

Common Forms of Manipulation

• One of the most used forms of manipulation is someone making you think they are better or above you. They might treat you as if you are a child or throw condescending looks or tones your way when you interact with them. Sometimes it can even go as far as to simply tell you that that they know better and their way is the best and only way. However, it happens, the message is clear, they're the 'superior,' and you are the 'inferior.' This is emotionally exhausting and beats down a person's self-esteem making it less likely that the manipulator will be challenged because at a point, you just stop speaking up because it never worked, to begin with.

• Making jokes at your expense is another common tactic used by manipulators. This is especially awful because it is not done in private. It is used as a method of putting someone down and making them feel small, and in order to do this, they need a group of people laughing. Sadly, this method has only grown in popularity because of the use of social media, where it is abundant. The jokes can range from physical attributes to how a person dresses, but either way, you are meant to be the butt of the joke and laughed at. When the manipulator is confronted, they usually come back with things like, "I was only kidding, you're too sensitive," making it seem like you are the problem.

• Sometimes all it takes is a look to manipulate someone. This might seem childish, but a facial expression has just as much power as words. Manipulators master the art of the death glare, the condescending head tilt, eye rolling, and shaking their head. Any facial expression or gesture that indicates to you, without words to back down. Even though this seems like something that you wouldn't fall victim to, it can and does happen. As a matter of fact, this type of manipulation can mean stop, you're wrong, you're ridiculous, and many other things that lower your self-esteem. And to make it worse, all of it with no words spoken.

•   Another common tactic is to simply ignore someone, for instance saying hello to everyone in the room except you; this can be demeaning and hurtful, not to mention also just embarrassing. Part of this is also acting bored, disinterested, and inconvenienced even when you are simply talking about everyday things. Going right along with this, they will often not answer any questions, phone calls, emails, text messages, and always seems unavailable. Many manipulators do this because they know it makes someone feel inferior, and they hope the person will go out of their way to understand what they did wrong and make up for it when in reality they did nothing wrong, and the manipulator is just using them for control and to gain something from the situation.

•   Guilt tripping is another common way for manipulators to get what they want, this comes out in the language they use which typically involves things such as, "I thought we were friends, I thought I could count on you, I can't believe how selfish you're being," and so on. This is a powerful way to exert control over the other person because they will wonder if what are saying is true and they will want to do everything in their power to fix it since they thought they were friends, and they will want to fix the friendship. That is when the demands come in from the manipulator, thus giving them what they wanted, at the expense of the other person's feelings.

• Some manipulative people choose to be deliberately difficult, making others cater to their whim in order to make them feel better. The more giving and agreeable you are to them, the more difficult they will be escalating the situation and blowing it out of proportion so they can have more control of the situation and wait until the other person goes out of their way to fix the situation.

• Overly complimenting people and telling them what they want to hear is also a great way for manipulators to get what they want, they are often called sweet talkers, and they mean nothing they say. They know people like to be complimented, and they use this to their advantage. They will tell you what you want to hear. However, it does not end there. They do this because they know it is one of the best ways to make friends, build trust, and then lower the other person's defenses, which is when the true manipulation can begin. They make it seem like all the praise they have been giving is worthy of something in return, and that is when they name their price. This tactic is also even more deplorable because the closer you are to someone, the easier it is for someone to manipulate you because there has been a friendship or relationship that involves trust that has already been cultivated.

The basic rules remain the same, but with different elements added to it to match the different types of circumstances. Even if they think they are masterminds and you are beneath them, the truth is, a manipulative person is not. They have just learned to use their behavior to get what they want to the point of not caring about others. They are not invisible; you can see them for what they are when you know what to look for.

There are also ways to determine whether or not you are in a manipulative friendship as well. Since manipulators use different relationships as a way to manipulate others, friendships are definitely not safe from these people either.

Manipulative Friends

•   Not listening: Friends should listen what each

other has to say, if you have a friend that expects you to listen to them, but does not return the favor, the chances are that friend has negative intentions. You might get the feeling that your friend is listening because they are looking at you, but instead of sincerity behind the action, it feels more like they are looking right through you. They are not retaining any of the information and are just going through the actions because they think they need to, in order to keep you in their lives. Everyone has bad days, so if this happens once, chances are your friend is just having a bad day, but it this continues to happen, then that is the red flag you were looking for.

• The gossiper: If you have a friend that never has anything nice to say, especially about the rest of the friend group, this too is a sign of manipulation. Manipulators like to stir the pot and will do nearly anything to do so. One of the ways they do this in a friend group is by keeping everyone on their toes by constantly spreading gossip and secrets.

• Out of touch: You might have that friend that only reaches out to you when they need something and seem to be missing in action when you do. This is not a healthy friendship because it sends the message that they only have time for you on their terms and your life doesn't really matter. This can cause self-doubt and low self-esteem. If you feel like you are constantly doing favors for this person and they never help you in return, this is not a true friendship.

•   Guilt: Using guilt within a friendship is different than most other relationships because there are other people involved. In cases of guilt, the manipulative person might claim that you have to help them after everything you've done for them. Another hallmark of a manipulative friend and guilt is rallying other people or at least making you think so. They might say things like "even so and so says I'm right and you're wrong." This serves as a way to isolate you, making you more likely to apologize and join their side, for whatever it is they are after.

•   Bossy: There is a difference from having a friend leader, the one who is just naturally good at organizing things and planning, and someone is intentionally bossy regardless of how the rest of the group feels. One of the best ways to understand out which is which, if someone gets mad at you if you don't like their idea, that is not a leader that is someone who is trying to be in control constantly, and that is classic manipulative behavior. They will ignore any reasonable suggestions that contradict what they want and will do anything they can to convince you to be on their side.

• So many favors: This can be tricky because friends do favors for one another and that is completely healthy and normal, it's good to have people to count on. However, if you have a friend that is constantly asking for favors and never seems to have the time to reciprocate, this is unhealthy. They will ask you to do things regardless of what is happening in your life, taking your time away from things that are important to you. This contributes to the feeling of a loss of self.

I

if you think that you have a manipulative friend, it can be difficult because other people are involved. So, one of the best things you can do, so as not to cause too much drama and split up a friend group, which could happen, is to distance yourself from that one person. You can do this by not doing the favors they ask you to do, or not asking them to do anything for you. Create plans and let everyone else know the game plan; this gives the manipulator less opportunity to want to change plans because everyone else will already be on board.

Having a manipulative person in a friend group is difficult

because it puts you in a tough spot if you are the only one who notices and knows what they're doing. The good news is, they are your friends too, and at some point, if the manipulative person begins acting in a way that puts too much strain on your friendships, it might be time to sit your friends down and tell them what you know. The best way to go about doing this, should it come to it, is to approach them as a group and calmly explain what manipulation is and how it works. Then use examples of how the friend in question has been treating not only you, but how you have seen them treat your other friends too.

Then, you will want to let them share their own personal experiences with the person as well, because sometimes saying it out loud will help understand how they have manipulated and hurt. Do not force them into saying anything; sometimes people are ashamed of how they have acted out of the ordinary because of the influence of someone else. That is why sharing your story first helps others to feel more comfortable talking about what has happened to them. Once everyone has talked about how they have been manipulated by that person, it is time for you and the rest of the group to decide what to do. Explain to them that confronting the person might just cause more issues and that if they have been manipulating everyone the whole time without caring about their feelings, that is probably not going to change.

More often than not, people are going to want to give someone another chance, and if that is what is decided, reiterate what manipulation is and how to tell when you are being manipulated. Encourage them to tell one another if the person engages in this type of behavior again. It is a good idea to make it clear that if they do, then the best thing for everyone is to stop being friends with them because even if the person apologizes, but makes no effort to change their behavior, nothing will change. It is for the best of everyone that the manipulator not be included anymore because that is what is healthiest.

Be A Positive Influence On Others

No matter which type of manipulation we talk about, Tricks and techniques are necessary to apply them in real life. It's true that those tricks which is used for negative manipulation are mostly decisive. But in the case of persuasion, the techniques can lead to a positive conclusion and to something great.

Now the question is how can manipulation be ethical or how can we differentiate between negative manipulation and persuasion. What are the steps or techniques?

What makes Persuasion Ethical?

Here's the facts about how can manipulation be ethical. First of all, most of us address these criteria as if it is a negative thing just because of the use of manipulation. The reality is, every single existence has two aspects, one is bright and another is dark side. The value of everything depends on our way of acting upon them, manipulation can be used for both good and evil purpose. The user is on the driving seat, so if it is driven through the dark path, not the method of manipulation but the user of it is to blame. It is our goal to manipulate anyone only to bring good results. If we want, we can apply a series of negative manipulation with a goal to deceive someone and make them do what we want. Or we can concentrate on the betterment of others. On that note, the right choice differentiates between the positive and negative sides. This is what makes manipulation a critical thing to practice.

Why Positive Manipulation methods are used

Positive manipulation or persuasion method can be so much helpful for the self-development of any individual. There are so many self-development skills based on which, a person can improve his/her life. There also are many situations where manipulation methods are being used. All those reasons and facts are described below.

Influence: Ethical manipulation is basically fully depended on influence. Influencing other individuals according to their need or influencing someone you know to do something for the betterment of that person, influencing to change habits, behavior all these are beneficial for the society and to improve social communication. In our daily life none can pass a single day without any influence. With or without our knowledge, we are being influenced by others and various desirable things in every aspect and almost always. Being influenced by good things are always appreciated. For example, if an addict quits being influenced by a good person, or you become influenced by the idea of buying a new iPhone-XI can drive you to earn more money. You can see both ideas are beneficial.

Persuasion: There are many times in our life when we face difficulties to make certain decisions or to deal with someone. Suppose it is your co-worker who does not agree with whatever you said, or any decision you have made. What are you supposed to do? The answer is you need to persuade that person by reasoning, or by making him see the benefits of doing what you decided. As long as the argument you are having remains honest, it falls within the criteria of persuasion.

Inspiration: Inspiration is something which is so much helpful if someone wants to manipulate anyone. Suppose someone is playing video games. If he/she keeps winning in the game, he/she gets inspired to play more. Or in the case of a depressed individual, he/she she needs inspiration and motivation in order to get back at the race of life. Inspiring someone to do something either good or bad is basic manipulation tactic.

Unity: Humans have a need of manipulation with almost everyone in their life. It can be someone they just met or someone they have known for a long time, like family members or friends. In the case of a stranger you just need to be logical but to manipulate someone you have known for a long time, unity is necessary. Suppose you want to propose a trip to Las Vegas upcoming summer. Now if your friends do not trust you, they most probably would not want to go. On the other hand, if you had built unity among your circle, they would trust you more, therefore agree to join you. Same goes for family relations. Unity is built upon trust. If someone does not trust you, he/she will not listen to you. How can you manipulate someone who will not listen to you?

For Self Defense: There are so many advantages of learning about the ethical manipulation. This can not only help you carry out your duties but also it can help you to defend yourself. There could be some situation where you need to defend yourself. Suppose someone alleged you about a certain matter as a negative view. Or maybe someone wants to pick a fight with you just because he/she feels like it. What can you do about it? Now if you know manipulation tricks, you can reason with him/her, if that does not work, you can make others around you to judge the situation and have them support you. So, if you know about ethical manipulation, you can easily defend yourself without any worries.

Reasons behind Compliance Manipulation's Ineffectiveness

At this part of the book, we are going to discuss some of the ethical manipulation techniques which can be used in every kind of situation. But in order to use these techniques, we must need to have the full understanding of the topic persuasion. This is usually important to become aware of, since persuasion can easily get confused with pressuring others into conformity. The second option is often focused only on changing the actions of other people by force or blackmailing, while persuasion techniques try to receive persons or groups to look and believe confidently about the thoughts or activities you would like for them to possess.

Manipulation for Compliance: There are lots of ways to manipulate people into complying with your ideas. Some illustrations of this are certainly not threats of legal action if you don't follow laws and regulations, neither is parents intimidating their child with punishment for not doing what they were told. These are not exampling of people complying, rather forcefully making others do something. Making a deal is a good example of people complying. Someone agreeing to do something for in exchange for something is the elaborated version of what I just said. Imagine your child refusing to complete his home task, you know he loves chocolate. Now if you offer to buy him chocolate only if he does his homework, there is a very good chance that he would listen to you now. Because he wants chocolate, and he knows to get chocolate he needs to complete his homework. Therefore, he complies. This can be applied on a much larger and much serious scale too.

Resentment and a Lack of Motivation: The problem with the type of techniques listed above is that without the greed or any benefit, individuals would not agree with or follow you. In addition to this, none relishes being negatively changed, signifying that they happen to become substantially even more extreme. They are most likely to search your replacement, once they discover what their normal spending criteria is. Lamentably, this sort of tricks nowadays is normally rampant, but although at some instances, it's absolutely is an amazingly top-notch or strong program.

When you look back again at being manipulated into compliance, perhaps simply by authorities at institution, bosses at work, or your own parents when you were young, you would feel as if you were used. It generally is not a very good feeling. In addition to that, it often causes negative emotions and interactions, and this is normally because it is structured on dread, rather than free of charge will and decision. How is it normally imaginable to get people to hold out what you would like them to hold out of their exceptional volition? They must make the decision themselves if they happen to plan to continue choosing it.

Using NLP and Creating Agreement for Successful Positive Manipulation

As we know from the discussions earlier, NLP and manipulation are inter related and those techniques can be applied on every kinds of people in order to gain succession. In the process of ethical or positive manipulation, it is not that much easy to apply manipulation and NLP on all the people.

Here are some factors and elements of NLP which can be used for successful positive manipulation.

Connect: Persuasion comes up with a view to connect

with the individuals as this is one of the most important way of knowing other people. As we all know there are so many factors regarding ethical manipulation. The practice of connecting with others makes the process of persuasion pretty much easier. It also helps to blend in with all the people who are around the individual you are trying to persuade. In the regular life of any person, there are so many people they might need to stay with, they might need to blend in with. This certain skill called connecting is unavoidable for all of them.

Trust: Trust is something which is not that much easy for anyone to gain but so much easier to lose. None can ever try to persuade anyone without this certain quality. To be exact, whenever anyone tries to get close to anyone, they must be trustworthy. This certain quality gives us the power to do whatever we want to do, whenever we want to do. Here is an example of the importance of trust. Suppose you want to get close to a certain person for the betterment of that person or because you care about the person. That person isn't going to listen to your words, unless that person has the faith /trust upon you. This is one of those Neuro-Linguistic methods which is a must for the ethical manipulation.

Breaking Patterns: In addition to building any

relationship, additional NLP methods exist for strong subliminal influence. One case in point of this is usually utilizing issues to re-direct someone's concentration or focus to something else, or to snooze mental habits. Issues which need to be ignored because they are hard to provide answers to. Our intellects quickly prefer to make an effort to fix issues even before they are asked.

Storytelling and Metaphors: By the term storytelling and metaphors, we understand very little. It may be hard to understand what we are trying to indicate. Here are the details for those term, when you are in the middle of the persuasion technique, you are that certain person who have the ability to make your subject be persuaded with some stories. Suppose you are practicing persuasion on a certain person you love and want changed. You are also trustworthy to that person. When you are in a position like that, you can tell a story similar to that person's story except for the details you want changed, then you can easily make the person understand which is right and wrong, why what needs to be done and which should not be done. On the other hand, metaphors have the same ability to change or persuade any people through the metaphorical descriptions.

Set a Goal: Nothing can be done without a certain vision

or goal. A goal is a target for which a person needs to put effort and walk onward. As referred in psychology, we can easily define goal as certain desire to attend and plan. For the purpose of persuasion, it is necessary to set a certain goal according which people needs to charge forward. Persuasion is depended on the neuro linguistic fact of the goal.

Get Confident and Passionate: Become enthusiastic about your technique, products, thought, or strategy. Do not forget to show passion applying your tactics. Willpower can undoubtedly be contagious and solid for salesmanship. Confidence is the key. This can often accomplish by emotionally attaching with whatever confident factors and rewards you happen to be producing with your thoughts.

It is crucial to get dismissed up, but also important to shake it off and represent confidently. In addition to this, giving logical perspectives is also helpful when it comes to ethical head game titles and persuading persons. Preserve in your head that individuals quite frequently utilize their selections based primarily on excitement, and in the long term justify those selections utilizing rational reasons. Showing interest to both of these is usually generally your best wager.

Be Upfront and Ask Directly: Another technique is to simply ask directly for whatever it is that you want. This might mean an evening out, seeking an individual to obtain your products, or prodding them to sign up for something. If you do not converse to, you will pretty much under no circumstances, discover out! An entire great deal of conditions, individuals very easily would not actually know very well what to bring out, and providing an action, believe, or choice can come to end up being useful for everyone operating.

Practice all of the know-how explained above to have an impact on salesmanship. Know how to develop and grow into strong potential. Staying excellent with salesmanship and legal steps is normally structured with the understanding of the cosmetic foundations of salesmanship. Practice a lot to able to fluently apply them. Keeping yourself smart with knowledge of salesmanship and steps tactics, can effectively defend you against persons making an attempt to employ them adversely against you.

How To Defend Yourself From Manipulation

We are indeed human at the end of the day. It is because of this very reason that we get to dwell allot on the opinion of others in everything that we do. We always desire and adore getting validation from others so that we can subconsciously decide whether we shall be depressed. In this age of the millennial, the norm has become to just brag about their wealth on social media. A lot of these bragging are often than not the truth. This ultimately leads to one having a loose relationship with reality. Self-deception of this type can dig deep into the human spicy, that a victim of these may one day wake up and realize that their perfect world is only existent within their maids. Depression will closely follow suit. The first step to attempting to defend yourself from manipulation and persuasion is confronting the situation and taking the stance of breaking off any illusions you may have. You will not be able to proceed normally with your life. You have to be wary of the fact that you are in control of your own choices. Then make the conscious choice of seeing things for what they are. That deal, which seems too good to be true, could actually be just that... too good to be true. The other thing you should follow is to definitely trust your instincts. There are times that a lie has been told to you in the most skilled way imaginable, that you will end up believing. But you can feel an imbalance on some instinctive level between what should be, what is, and then what is being projected onto you. There may be no physical signs to show that hey, something is wrong, but you feel something is wrong. The following important thing when you ask questions is to listen to the responses. This may sound somewhat unbelievable because you'll listen to the answers. The truth is that our self-disappointment can make us choose the answers we receive. We tell ourselves that we listen, but we only pay attention to the answers we want to hear rather than to the answers we receive. You may have broken the illusions around you, but some of you are still clinging to the comfort of those illusions. The pain of confronting the situation would prevent you from listening to the real answers to your questions. Actual listening requires a certain sense of detachment, but this time around not from reality. You have to get rid of your emotions. Your detachment from our emotions would lead you to the following step, which would logically process the new information. It can complicate situations more than they already are to act irrationally. It makes your exit strategy so much difficult to let all the emotions simmer and spring to the surface. When you face the truth, the irrational part of you may want you to let it all go hell. Your rightly justified anger can inspire you to take steps to calm your emotions in the short term. But you may come to regret these actions in the long term. I'm not saying that you should deny your emotions; I'm not saying that you do not act on these emotions.

Act quickly

It's great that you have come to terms with the reality of things. But defense against these dark manipulative tactics entail so much more. While attempting to defend you from the claws of these manipulators, is often intense and exhilarating at first. This intensity of these emotions may cause one to slowly slide into denial. The more you delay in taking any action is usually what accelerates the onset of this denial, and when it happens, there are high chances that you might relapse and end up getting trapped in the same web. This can be avoided by taking action immediately you realize that someone is trying to manipulate you. This can present itself in the simplest of ways like when informing a close friend of some reality of the particular situation may be all that's needed so set in motion a series of events that will eventually lead to your freedom. You should know that the fabric of illusion is made from tougher material than glass after making the choice to act. The illusion could work its way back into your heart with your emotions in high gear by using fragments of your emotions to fix it. When a liar is caught in a lie, he or she may attempt to recruit others to enforce that lie when they feel that they are no longer holding you. A deceptive partner with whom you have recently broken things off would at this point try to use the other mutual relationships in your life to change your mind. If you want to get out of this unscathed, you will need both your logic and instincts. Although the truth of the situation is that when you discover that you've been lied to consistently, you become emotionally scarred, so the issue of leaving the situation unscathed becomes silent. Priority should be given, however, to take the route that allows you to leave this toxic situation without harming yourself further. You're all over the place emotionally. Rage, anger, hurt, and deception is the iceberg's tip. But logically, you need to think. Keep your head above the water and warn yourself.

Get help fast

When you're trapped by other people's manipulations, confusion is one of the emotions you'd experience. This helps cloud your rational thinking and leaves you feeling helpless. You might even question the reality of what you are facing at this point. It would lead to denial if you continue to entertain these doubts. You're probably going to want to conclude you've got the whole situation wrong. That you misunderstood some things and came to the wrong conclusion. Such thinking would drive back to the manipulator's arms. Resist the urge to give in by receiving a second opinion. People go to another doctor in a health crisis to get a second opinion. This is to remove any iota of doubt about the first diagnosis that you may have and to affirm the best treatment course for you.

Similarly, getting another person's opinion can help you discern the truth of the situation and what might be your following steps. Just remember, it's better to go to someone who has proved countless times they're interested in your best. The following step is to confront the perpetrator if you have the help you need. For this, I suggest you choose the scene or location. Choose a place you know that gives you the upper hand. On your part, that would require some careful planning. If the perpetrator exists in the cyber world, especially if the person swindled you of your money, you would have to involve the police and the relevant authorities. Do some of your own investigations to ascertain the truth. After you face the perpetrator and take the necessary steps to get out of the situation, you must start the healing process quickly.

The scale and gravity to which you were hurt, manipulated or abused do not matter. You must be able to walk past it and wait until you can "heal" your wounds, rather than sitting on your couch and reliving the past. If you don't do anything about it, an unhealthy scab could form over the wound, which would make you as vulnerable if not more than you had experienced. Speak to a counsellor, attend therapy, and take an active part in facilitating the healing process, whatever you choose to do. It won't happen overnight, but you are sure that you get closer to improving every day and every step you take in therapy.

Trust your instincts

While your brain interprets signals based on facts, logic, and sometimes experience, your heart works in the opposite direction by screening information through an emotional filter. The only thing that picks up vibrations is your gut instinct, which neither the heart nor the brain can pick on. And if you can groom to the point where you recognize your inner voice and are trained to react to it, you will lower your chances of being seduced by people trying to work on you with their manipulative will. To begin with, it's hard to recognize this voice. And that's because we allowed voices of doubt, self-discrimination as well as the critics loud voices within and without drowning out our authentic voice over the course of our lives. Your survival depends on this voice or instinct. So, trust that when it kicks in, your brain neurons can still process things in your immediate vicinity.

Some people call it intuition, and some refer to it as instinct, especially when it comes to relationships, they are undoubtedly the same thing. You must accept that it may not always make logical sense to start trusting your instincts. If you've ever been in the middle of doing something and experienced the feeling of being watched all of a sudden, then you know what I mean. You don't have eyes at the back of your head, there's no one else with you in the room, but you get the tiny shiver running down your spine and the "sudden knowledge" you're watching. That's what I'm talking about. The first step to connect with your instinct is to decode your mind with the voices you've let in. With meditation, you can do this. Forget the chatter of "he said, she said." Concentrate on your center. You are the voice you know. Then, be careful about your thoughts. Don't just throw away the eclectic monologs in your head. Rather go with the thoughts flow.

Why do you think of a certain person in some way? How do you feel so deeply about this person, even if you only knew each other for a few days? What's that nagging feeling about this other person that you have? You get more tuned to your intuition as you explore your thoughts and understand when your instincts kick and how to react to it. You may need to learn to take a step back to pause and think if you are the kind of person who prefers to make spur decisions at the moment. This moment in which you pause gives you the opportunity to really reflect on your decisions and evaluate them. The following part is a hard part and it couldn't be followed by many people. Unfortunately, you can't skip or navigate around this step. This part has to do with trust. You need to be open to the idea of trusting yourself and trusting others to be able to trust your instinct. Your failure to trust others would just make you paranoid, and it's not your instincts that kick when you're paranoid. It's the fear of you. Fear tends to turn every molehill into a hill. You must let go of your fear, embrace confidence, and let that lead in your new relationships. You are better able to hear the voice inside without the roadblocks put up by fear in your mind. Finally, your priorities need to be re-evaluated. If your mind is at the forefront of money and material possessions, you may not be able to see the past. Any interaction you have with people would be interpreted as people trying to take advantage of you, and if you dwell on that frequently enough, it will soon become your reality. You know how you attract into your life what you think of. If you're constantly thinking about material wealth, you're only going to attract people who think like you. Using this as a guide, look at all your relationships with this new hindsight; the old, the new, and the perspective. Don't enter a relationship that expects to be played. Be open when you approach them, whether it's a business relationship, a romantic relationship or even a regular acquaintance. You can get the right feedback about them from your intuition. Do not step into this thinking, too, that your gut will tell you to run in the opposite direction when you meet suspect people.

Part 2 Persuasion

Introduction

In life, anywhere you look, there are chances to be persuaded. Whether it is the billboard you pass on your way to work, the person you text most often, or even the lover with whom you share children, these things and people can be influential and persuasive. While it is important to know how others may be influencing you, it is an entirely different concept to figure out how to influence others.

Persuasion and influence are an art, and like art, they take practice. After you have completed this reading, you will better understand persuasion. However, you may not be able to go out and convince everyone of what you want them to do right away. It takes time, but if you stay committed to your goals and dedicated to your intentions, you will become a master persuader in no time.

The aim of persuasion is not to manipulate but to

bring people to decisions that are in their best interest and to help further worthwhile causes. These are causes that are beneficial and bring value to society. While you will most likely benefit from the persuasion tactics in which you choose to partake, you should ensure that they are beneficial for other parties involved as well.

If you continue to take from people but never give back, this behavior may haunt you one day. Persuasion and influence should be viewed in a positive light as tools that help people, not as a means of hurting others.

The foundation for the practice of influence and persuasion is understanding human psychology, how people make decisions, and how they are wired. Everyone is different, so the ways that you decide to persuade them will differ as well. If you are knowledgeable about psychology, you will have an easier time differentiating individuals and understanding what persuasion tactics are best used on them.

From there, techniques and practices can be pursued sincerely. If you are genuine with intention and actually want to help people, it will be easy to adopt the methods and strategies of some excellent influencers and persuaders. Remember that it is going to take some trial and error, and not everyone will agree with your viewpoint right away. Make sure that you are in a mindset where you are ready to take criticism and willing to accept the fact that some people just will not be persuaded.

Learning starts by making sure that you are aware of the power of influence and persuasion. They can be harmful tools if they are put into the wrong hands, and as you are reading these words, a few people probably come to mind right away. In order to ensure that you are not using these methods of influence improperly, we are going to take you through negative stereotypes to ensure that you are not someone who is going to take advantage of anyone.

When used correctly, persuasion and influence can elicit positive change in groups of people rather than just from individual to individual. Connecting with people on a general level and determining mutual interests will be helpful in ensuring you are someone who can easily persuade others.

When you understand that these methods can be very helpful in your life, you can start to learn ways in which you can implement the best practices into your everyday activity. There are many benefits and advantages to being a persuasive person. The most obvious one is that you will be better at getting what you want.

From there, you will realize that you have more confidence, which can seriously reduce stress and anxiety. By reducing these things alone, you are going to feel much better; you will have the power needed to be the person you have always wanted to be.

It is important to know the difference between influence and persuasion. They are related, and you cannot have one without the other. However, the terms are not interchangeable. One means a specific moment, and the other is in reference to a more prolonged period of encouragement.

Once you learn how to be persuasive, you will most likely be happier altogether. Instead of sitting silently in the background, you will be able to use your voice to speak up for what matters. Though it might seem scary at times, you are going to become the person you have always admired; an influential and inspirational leader who knows what it takes to be successful. Your confidence will keep building over time, especially the more you practice refining your skills.

Examples are provided, but remember to apply the methods and techniques specifically to your situation. We are all different, and our levels of expertise differ as well. You will be confronting those you wish to persuade, so ensure that you are personalizing your strategies to your individual life. That is what being a persuasive influencer is all about!

Principles Of Persuasion

When we discuss manipulation and persuasion, it usually comes down to a difference of intent. For instance, is the person who is persuading you to do something that will benefit both you and them? If so, that's the classic win-win scenario, and we could say that persuasion was used to help you come to the right decision.

But what if the same person gets you to do something that benefits him, but leaves you worse off? That would be characterized as manipulation, and that type of persuasion happens all of the time, too. You may have done it yourself without really realizing it, and not felt too good about it afterward.

Persuasion can be used for all kinds of purposes,

both good and evil. People can manipulate you into giving them your money, your time, your faith, your talent, and provide you with nothing in return. Or they can persuade you into giving of all of these things and leave you better off in the end. And sometimes, the lines aren't so clearly drawn.

Ultimately, everyone makes their own decisions. By being aware of persuasion techniques, you can more successfully analyze your motivations and make sure that what you are doing benefits both you and others.

Today's Pervasive Persuasion

Persuasion is also an important topic today because we are contacted by more and more sophisticated methods of persuasion than ever before. Persuasion comes at us in all forms, at a velocity never even possible before. I'm sure you can guess the cause of this increased persuasion. That's right! It's called The Internet.

Never before have people had direct access to the tools of mass communication. You can pick up your smartphone and start broadcasting live right now, with just a few clicks. You can start typing and send your views to millions of people around the world. Or you can post a picture of that adorable thing your cat just did to your partner to brighten their day at work. And all of the people you are reaching can get that information instantly because they probably have a smartphone or computer or screen nearby that they are looking at, and you have access to that network. This type of reach and access was unheard of only a decade or two ago. Today, this connection is commonplace and growing.

The Principles of Persuasion

Since that book, many researchers have created experiments to test these theories with surprisingly consistent results. The bottom line is that we humans seem to be hard-wired to behave in certain ways given certain circumstances. Using various methods to trigger those responses that we want, we can cause the outcomes that we want.

The 6 Principles Of Persuasion

Reciprocation

Give something to get something, right? Remember the story of the chicken who planted grain so that her chicks could eat? She asked for help to sow the grain, to keep the field clean from weeds, to harvest the grain and finally, to make the bread. She asked her neighbors and friends to help, but in the end, no one was interested until the bread was hot and ready to eat. Since her neighbors had not given her anything in the form of help, she was not inclined to give them any of the final product.

That give and take is the first principal of getting along in life, and it's known as one of the foundational principals of persuasion as well. Reciprocity merely means that if you give someone something, they are more likely to give you something in return.

Commitment and Consistency

We, humans, have a "reality" surrounding us at all times. I put this "reality" in quotes because it is a reality of our creation.

Our brains have an innate ability to tell stories, and we tell ourselves stories all of the time. We tell ourselves stories of the type of person we believe we are, and how we behave feeds into that story. When presented with a choice, you make that choice based on the story of who you are. One of the options looks "right" to us because making that choice is consistent with what we believe a person like us would do.

Social Proof

This core persuasion principle is also sometimes referred to as Consensus. We have told ourselves a story of what we believe we are, what we stand for, and the kind of person we are. To reinforce that story, we look at how other people behave for Social Proof of how people like us should react in a particular situation.

Now more than ever, the Internet has created countless places where we can go for this type of reinforcement. Some of that reinforcement is legitimate, some not so much. All of it is used as a powerful tool for persuasion, as we'll find out going forward.

Authority

Now once we have decided on the type of person we are and we've assembled with the kinds of people we believe reinforce that identity; the next step is to seek out knowledgeable people to reinforce what we've told ourselves to be true. That's where the idea of Authority takes hold.

As sane people, we are likely to take the advice of people who appear to have more knowledge about a subject than we do. That is certainly necessary. No one can know everything, not even with smartphones and Google just a tap away. We seek out the advice of people who know more about a subject than we do.

Liking

Liking is one of those core principles that seems obvious, but yet it needs definition since it is at the hub of all types of persuasion. Liking, simply put, means that you are much more likely to be persuaded by someone that you like.

If you don't like someone, are you going to take their advice? Probably not. We humans are wired to make snap judgments about almost every situation we get into, and one of the simplest decisions to make is whether we like someone or not. Every person you meet triggers a feeling instantly of comfort or wariness. This was a survival skill in the early days of our evolution, and it still holds sway today, as we'll see.

Scarcity

Speaking of evolution's early days, our final persuasion principal is an obvious holdover from the early days of staying alive. Scarcity makes things more valuable to us, so when something seems like it is limited in quantity, we are more likely to want it.

Sand is commonplace; gold is not. Which would

you rather have? Or more to the point, what does all humankind want more? It most certainly used to be food that was so valuable, so that early man found ways to preserve food when it was abundant so that it would be around when food got scarce.

Survival depends on specific resources that can be in short supply, so humans are naturally prone to try and save and hang on to that which is not always available. Since this is core hardwiring in our brains, we'll see that this is an often-used method of persuasion today.

Art Of Persuasion

Persuasion is a theme of dark psychology that can be said to share quite a bit of similarity to manipulation. This is because they are both deployed in order to influence the motivations, behaviors, attitudes, and beliefs of a particular victim. There are a number of reasons why we adopt persuasion into our everyday lives, but the main one would have to be to get people with different ideas on the same page. In company, for instance, the persuasion method will be used to alter the attitude of a person towards an item, concept, or a particular event that is taking place. Either written or spoken phrases will be used during the process to express the other person's thinking, emotions, or data. Another common instance you can use persuasion is to fulfil a private benefit. This would include either advocacy for trial when providing a pitch for sales or during an election campaign. Although none of these are deemed to be good or evil, they are still used to affect the listener to behave or believe in some manner.

One understanding of persuasion is that it utilizes one's private or positional resources to alter other people's attitudes or behaviors. Persuasion is a type of mind control that is constantly being used in society. You may attempt to convince them to believe the same way you do when you speak to someone about politics. You are persuaded to vote a certain way when you listen to a political campaign. There's a lot of persuasion going on when someone is attempting to sell you a fresh item. This form of mind control is so prevalent that most people don't even know it's happening at all to them. The problem will arise when someone takes the time to convince you to believe ideals and values that do not suit your own value system. There are many distinct types of persuasion available. Not all of them have a bad intention, but they will all work to get the subject to change their minds about something. When a political candidate arrives on television, on Election Day they try to get the topic, or the voter, to vote on the ballot a certain way. The company that submitted that advertisement is attempting to get the victim to buy that item when you see a commercial on television or online. All of these are kinds of persuasion that are bent on attempting to modify the way they believe about the victim. To get the victim to modify their way of thinking. Dark persuasion has no moral motivation whatsoever. The motivation is rather amoral and sometimes largely immoral. If beneficial conviction is understandable as assisting individuals to help themselves, dark persuasion can be seen as a mechanism by which individuals behave against their own self-interest. Sometimes people make it reluctantly, knowing that they may not make the best choice, but are keen to stop the continuous persuasion efforts. On other occasions, the best dark persuaders can make someone think they act wisely when they actually do just the opposite.

So, what are the primary reasons for these dark persuaders? It depends on the type of person who persuades. Some people try to convince others to serve their own interests. Others do pure harm by the sole malicious intent. They may not profit from persuading anyone, but they do it anyhow, solely in order to bring pain to their victims. Others just appreciate the feeling of control provided by dark persuasion.

The result of dark persuasion is also different from positive persuasion. Positive persuasion usually results in one of three scenarios: benefit of the persuaded, benefit for the persuader and the persuaded or mutual benefit for the persuaded individual and a third party. All these results have a positive result for the person to be convinced. Sometimes other people benefit, sometimes they don't. However, there is no situation where only the manipulator benefits.

Dark persuasion has a very distinct set of results. The persuader always advantages either immediately or by his distorted need for control and impact. The persuaded individual is against their own self-interest and is not persuaded. Finally, not only do the most qualified dark persuaders' damage their victims, but they also damage others. Take a dark persuader who tells somebody to commit suicide so they can take advantage of an insurance policy. The persuader not only won financially, but also the victim lost his life and hurt everyone who knew or cared for them.

Who are these individuals who often tend to use dark persuasion? The main characteristic of a dark persuader is either indifference or an inability to be concerned about the impact of persuasion on others. They are either completely narcissistic and regard their own requirements to be far more essential than the requirements of others or they are sociopathic and unable to even understand the notion of the feelings of others. In a partnership, you often discover dark persuasion. In the worst case scenario, both partners are inclined to persuade the other darkly. The connection can be regarded psychologically abusive if such efforts are persistent and durable. Some instances of dark relationships include not allowing the other partner to take fresh jobs or to take private pleasure. The obscure persuader will persuade the victim to act "for the sake of friendship." The victim merely hurts himself and the relationship in fact. The connection is being damaged as the dark persuader gains greater assurance that his victims can be manipulated.

Elements of persuasion

Like other types of control, some components are to be observed when it comes to persuasion. These components assist to precisely identify which persuasion makes it clearer. The ability to convince others is one salient feature that distinguishes persuasion from all other themes of dark psychology since the victim is in most cases allowed to make choices out of their own will, I as much as persuasion tactics will sooner work towards changing his will to that of the persuader. The topic can choose the manner they want to believe, whether or not they want to buy a product, or whether they believe the proof behind the persuasion is powerful enough to alter their minds. There are a few components in persuasion that assist to further describe what is while giving us a deeper understanding of this enigmatic theme.

The first element of this theme is that persuasion is often symbolic. What this means is that persuasion utilizes words, sound as well as images so as to get the message across to the specific victim. The logic behind this is quite simple really. For one individual to be able to persuade another into acting in a particular way, they will need to show them why they should act in said way and not vice versa. This is best achieved by using word sounds or various images you can use sentences to start a debate or argument to prove your point. Pictures are a great way to show the evidence needed to persuade someone to go one way or the other. Some nonverbal signs are possible, but they are not as effective as using words and images

The second key is that persuasion will be used deliberately to affect how others act or think. This one is quite obvious; you don't use persuasion to get them to change if you don't deliberately try to affect others. In order to get the topic to believe the same way they do, the persuader will attempt distinct strategies. This could be as easy as having a discussion with them or presenting proof supporting their point of perspective. On the other hand, to change the mind of the subject, it could involve much more and include more deceptive forms.

The distinctive thing about persuasion is that it enables some type of free will for the topic. In this way, the topic is permitted to create its own decision. For the most part, they don't have to go for it, no matter how hard somebody tries to persuade them of something. The subject might hear about the best car to buy a thousand commercials, but if they don't like that brand or don't need a new vehicle at that time, they won't go out and buy it. If the subject is against abortion, how many people will come out and say how great abortion is, it's not likely that the subject will change their minds This enables much more freedom of choice than is found in the other types of mind control, which could explain why when questioned, many individuals do not see this as a kind of mind control. Persuasion is a type of mind control that can take place in many respects. While brainwashing, hypnosis and manipulation must happen face-to-face, and in some instances in full isolation, persuasion may happen otherwise.

Examples of persuasion can be found everywhere,

including when you talk to individuals you know, on the Internet, on radio and television. It is also feasible to deliver persuasive messages by nonverbal and verbal means; although when verbal methods are used it is much more efficient

Subliminal persuasion

The word "subliminal" means underneath our consciousness. Subliminal persuasion means an advertising message that is displayed below the threshold of awareness or consumer awareness in order to persuade, persuade or help people change their minds without making them aware of what is going on. This is about affecting individuals with more than words. Some of the subliminal methods of persuasion impact our stimuli with smell, eyesight, sound, touch, and taste. There are mainly 3 subliminal methods of persuasion to affect anyone. They are

•   Building a relationship-building relationship makes the other person feel comfortable. This will open up the other individual more. This can be accomplished through a healthy observation strength that matches their mood or state. This helps create confidence

•   Power of discussion–the power of a powerful

convincing person is much connected to an advertiser's conversion. The correct words and inflections help you to be openly straightforward.

• Suggestive power-Associating useful and desirable stuff in discussion or interaction enables an individual to become more open to fresh thoughts.

Suggestion and emotional intelligence

This stage may be described as having one central and dominant idea focused on the participant's conscious mind, which was to stimulate or decrease the physiological performance of the various regions within the participant's body. Sooner, the use of different non-verbal and verbal suggestions was increasingly emphasized in order to convince the participant easily.

Basic Persuasion techniques

There are techniques that can be utilized so as to make persuasion more successful. All victims are usually presented with different forms of persuasion on a daily basis. A food manufacturing plant will work on getting their victims to purchase a new product, while a movie company will focus on persuading their victims to watch their latest movie projects. There are three main techniques of persuasion that have been prevalent since the birth of this theme.

Create a need

This is one of the techniques that are often deployed by the manipulator so as to be able to get the victim to change their way of thinking. This creates a need or rather appeals to a need that is already pre-existing within the victim. If it is executed in a skilled way, the victim will be eating out of the persuader's palm in no time. What this means is that the manipulator will need to tap into the fundamental needs of their victim like for example their need for self-actualization. This technique will in most casework so well for the manipulator because the victim is actually going to need these things. Food for example is usually something that we as humans need in order to survive and prolonged lack will pause as a big problem. If the agent can convince the subject that their store is the best, or if they can get more food or shelter by switching their beliefs, there is a higher chance of success.

Utilizing illustrative and words

The choice of words one chooses to use comes a long way in the success of using persuasion. There are many ways in which you can phrase sentences when actually talking about one thing. Saying the right words in the right way is what will make all the difference when attempting to use persuasion.

Tricks used by mass media and advertising

The media use two main methods which they use to persuade the masses. First is through the use of images, as well as the use of sounds.

Media persuasion by use of images

Our sighs and visual processing areas of the brain are very powerful. Just think about it for a minute, have you ever thought of a person without ending up picturing how they look? It is because of this that makes imagery and visual manipulation a preferred method by the media. Companies will often include split-second images of their product or individual inserted into an advertisement that seems quite innocent on the face value. This usually a form of subliminal persuasion. These split-second images that are usually assumed for the most part usually end up taking some form of control of the victim, which persuades them to purchase that particular service.

Media persuasion by the use of sound

Sound is yet another trick that is used by media in the persuasion of unsuspecting victims. Some people usually underestimate the powers that exist within the sound. But answer me this, how many times have you heard a song somewhere only to have it loops through your mind continuously? Songs usually have an influence on us even though we are not aware of it despite knowing you are listening to it. This is what the media tend to exploit in their quest for persuasion of the masses. There will often be a number of phrases skillfully hidden, and repeated in an advertisement song that will most likely convince you to be inclined to prefer one company over the other. An example of this is seen at McDonald's. The melody 'I'm loving it 'is often repeated in a manner that persuades the victims to constantly purchase their meals.

Indicators That You're A Victim Of Manipulation

Once manipulation is identified, the next step is to get through it. Overcoming manipulation can be very challenging. In some cases, a 60 year-old-man might realize just now that his 85 year-old-mother is manipulative. They might never get through their issues, but they should still be confronted. Manipulation takes a part of both the abuser and the victim. It can ruin people's lives, altering the direction they take and affecting the rest of their years. Manipulation can be hard to identify and even harder to overcome.

It can be done, and it should be attempted to get through. In a relationship based around manipulation, there might not be any coming back. Sometimes, people might just have to break up. You might have to get a divorce or stop calling your mom. It takes two people to partake in a manipulative scenario. Not both people will end up identifying it as a manipulative situation, however. In that case, the person that realizes what's actually going on might just have to move on, the manipulator never realizing the damage they caused.

This can be a challenging part of overcoming manipulation. Usually, some instance of codependency formed, making it even harder to break away.

Hypnosis

If mind control is the best set of manipulation strategies for beginners to pick up and be able to learn quickly, then hypnosis is the next natural step in the process towards becoming a master of manipulation. In general, hypnosis lasts longer and is far more powerful than mind control is, although it also requires more skill to successfully pull off. While hypnosis has some concepts that overlap with mind control and brainwashing, it also has completely unique components, which can make it more challenging to learn. Hypnosis has a long a rich history, and today it is used in a wide variety of fields and industries, including in medicine, sports, psychotherapy, self-improvement, meditation and relaxation, forensics and criminal justice, art and literature, and the military. Of course, all instances of hypnosis share common characteristics no matter what context it is used in, and these same characteristics can come in handy when attempting to manipulate someone else. Having a good understanding of the principles and concepts of hypnosis can turn you from a mediocre manipulator into a highly skilled one.

The Hypnotic Trance

At its core, hypnosis is all about planting ideas into somebody else's subconsciousness in order to influence their consciousness. If you manage to infiltrate a person's subconsciousness with enough skill, they will not be aware of what you are doing, and will never know that you ever influenced them at all. The best way to access someone's subconsciousness is to coax them into a relaxed, meditative state known as a hypnotic trance. Getting your target into a trance is the most difficult part of the process of hypnosis, but once you finally manage to pull it off, you will have a much easier time successfully manipulating them. Putting your target into a trance allows for you to have direct access to their subconsciousness, as their consciousness will no longer be an active part of their mind for the duration of the trance. The trace is what separates hypnosis from mind control, and the ability to induce it in somebody else is what separates a beginner of manipulation from a budding expert.

The best way to think of a hypnotic trance is a form of deep relaxation. You are likely already familiar with the overall concept of the trace, due to portrayals of hypnosis in book, movies, and popular culture in general. Of course, in real life, you cannot put somebody else into a hypnotic trance simply by waving a watch in front of their face or by using a magical code phrase that will put them to sleep. Instead, putting someone into a hypnotic trance takes lots of time and skill, and it may not always work on every single person that you try it out on, especially when you are first starting to attempt to use it. In fact, for the best introduction to the hypnotic trance, you may want to find a friend who is willing to allow you to put them into a trance in order to practice doing it, or if you cannot find someone who is a willing participant, you can always put yourself into a hypnotic trance using this same method. If you fail at putting somebody into a trance, you are likely to face a negative reaction from that person, as they are likely to recognize suspicious behavior when they see it if they still have full awareness of their surroundings. This is why it is important that you practice this technique several times before attempting it on any outsiders, as you are far more likely to succeed in putting somebody into a hypnotic trance if you have some familiarity with how it already works.

Advanced Techniques and Suggestibility Testing

At this point we have learned about various methods of manipulation through neuro-linguistic programming and hypnosis. By now you are armed with a plethora of weapons to use on any given subject, and you are prepared defensively if someone attempts to use any of these tactics against you.

Suggestibility Testing

Many hypnotists will tell you that suggestibility testing is best left to the street performers and entertainment hypnotists. This may be true as it has limited viability in hypnotherapy but what many hypnotists don't think about is everyday manipulation. Suggestibility testing is vastly utilizable in the realm of conversational hypnosis and everyday hypnosis towards the ends of manipulation. So what it is?

Suggestibility testing can refer to any number of verbal or physical "feelers" that help the hypnotist determine whether or not their subject is a good target for hypnosis and manipulation. They can serve as a guide for one to determine how likely a subject will bend to their will. Some hypnotists use suggestibility training to determine how deep into a hypnotic trance their subjects are but our purposes will be a little different.

For our intents and purposes we will use suggestibility testing to find our subjects in the first place. The reason anyone would want to use suggestibility testing is to find the right subject for manipulation. The caveat with hypnotism, even conversational hypnosis, is that some people are more suggestible to others. In other words, some people are less likely to be inducted into hypnosis than others. For this reason Dark NLP practitioners often use suggestibility testing to have a better idea of who they can manipulate and who they might not be able to.

The reason you will want to learn these tests is essentially for efficiency. For example, you wouldn't want to use a lot of your time and effort trying to manipulate someone whom you've tested to have low suggestibility. It would just take too long and besides, there are tons of easily suggestible targets to choose from. In fact, it is estimated that as much as 80% of the population is in the average range of hypnotic suggestibility – meaning that up to 80% of the population can be successfully hypnotized with moderate effort.

That is why suggestibility testing is so useful for the Dark NLP practitioner. It gives a good guideline on who a prime subject might be and helps the practitioner avoid difficult subjects.

Suggestibility tests can be deployed fairly easily. Let's

take a look at some of the best methods for testing suggestibility.

The Light/Heavy Hands Technique

This method of suggestibility testing depends heavily on the concentration and that imagination of the subject. How keenly a person can bring their concentration and imagination into alignment is a very important factor. It will determine how susceptible they will be to actual hypnotic suggestion.

In this test you will be able to see a physical manifestation of their level of suggestion. It is sometimes called the book and balloon test as well and you will see why in just a moment. The idea behind this test is to see just how deeply one can delve into their own minds. The belief is that the body will react physically if someone is concentrating on something that they believe is true. If you see that your subject reacts bodily to the light/heavy hands technique then they are more than likely a prime target for Dark NLP and hypnosis. So here is what you are going to want to do:

Ask someone, or multiple people, to close their eyes and hold their arms straight out in front of them. Tell them to have one hand turned palm-up to the sky and one hand palm-down to the ground. Now tell them to imagine that in the hand that is facing toward the sky, they are carrying a watermelon. In the hand they have facing the ground, tell them that there are a bunch of helium balloons tied to their wrist.

Go into detail about the watermelon. They can smell it, feel its rind and most importantly, feel how heavy it is. With each passing moment their arms are getting more and more fatigued from the weight of the heavy watermelon. Meanwhile the arm with the balloons tied to it is getting lighter as the balloons are slowly and gently ascending towards the sky. What you should be doing while their eyes are closed is seeing if their arms are actually moving. If they are, then you've most likely found your subject.

The Amnesia Technique

The amnesia technique is a verbal test. In it you will ask the potential subject to forget about something for a period of time (it shouldn't be more than a few minutes). For example, you can ask your subject to forget the letter P. Tell them to pretend that the letter P never existed and to forget that you even told them to forget about it. Then ask them to recite the alphabet. People who are moderately or highly suggestible will skip over the letter P (or whatever letter you tell them to forget) and not even realize it. Once again, if the person you tried this test on skips over the letter you told them to forget, they may be a good subject to zone in on.

The Locked Hand Technique

The locked hand technique (also known as the hand clasp technique) is another physical test that the subject will have to be willing to participate in. Like the light/heavy hand technique, it will test just how deeply a person can concentrate on the words you are saying to them and what you are telling them to imagine. Ask your subject to clap their hands together and keep them together, palm to palm. Then tell them to interlace their fingers. Make sure that you maintain fixed eye-contact with them throughout this test and tell them to push their hands together as tightly as they can. Tell them to imagine their hands merging into one piece of solid flesh and bone. After a minute or two, tell them to stop pushing and try pulling their hands apart. Again, a potential manipulation subject will find it hard to pull their hands away from each other.

Know Your Worth

The first step in overcoming manipulation is for the victim to identify that they still have value. A manipulator likely took everything from their victim. They belittled them, ridiculed them, and made them feel as though what they thought didn't matter. In some situations, they might have even used gaslighting tactics to make their victims feel as though they're insane. It can be hard for a victim to then recognize just how much value they still have once they become aware of the manipulation.

It's important for everyone to know, no matter who is reading this, that you have worth. Everyone has value. No one deserves to be manipulated. No one deserves to feel as though they don't have any purpose, reason, or value. You have the right to be treated justly, and with respect from other people. You are allowed to express your emotions, feelings, wants, and opinions. No one else has the right to tell you how to feel. You set your own boundaries, and no one else gets to decide for you.

If you feel sad about something, that is completely valid. No one gets to decide if what they say hurts you or not. Not everyone might intentionally mean to hurt you, but that doesn't mean you're not allowed to still feel bad. You have the right to feel the way you do, and you have the same right to express those beliefs.

If you feel like you need to protect yourself, you are just in doing so. If you feel like your safety is being threatened, or someone is taking advantage of you, you have the right to remove yourself from that situation without guilt. No one gets to treat you badly, and though that can be hard for many of us to hear, it's the truth.

Manipulators aim to take these thoughts away. They want to deprive their victims of their rights in order to work towards getting what they want. This can't happen anymore. It's up to the manipulator's victims to now recognize their worth and stop the cycle of manipulation.

Don't Be Afraid to Keep Your Distance

Many people that feel as though they're being manipulated end up being too afraid to do anything about it. They have been stripped of their own thoughts and opinions, their own feelings invalidated and instead focus on how other people feel. Those that have been continually manipulated might be afraid to leave those that have hurt them. They've depended on those that abused them for so long they don't know where else to go.

You're allowed to keep your distance. You don't have to feel guilty about protecting yourself. It can be hard to separate yourself from a manipulator, especially in a romantic relationship. You might see the very weaknesses that cause their manipulative behavior. Maybe in a relationship, a boyfriend's dad was an abusive alcoholic, and it greatly hurt him. It also caused his violent manipulative behavior that led him to hitting his girlfriend on a few occasions. It's true that he has his own pain, but that doesn't mean he's allowed to inflict it on others. The girlfriend has every right to leave her boyfriend and find her own peace and protection.

Ask what is really lost by leaving the person that's manipulating you. More often than not, value in a relationship is placed on codependent tendencies. A person is afraid to leave not because they love their manipulator, but because they are afraid to be alone. It can be scary to be on your own, but mostly because manipulators put that idea in their victims in the first place. Manipulators will trick their victims into staying with them because deep down, they know that the victim will be just fine without them.

It's Not Your Job to Change Them

Once manipulation is recognized, the next step is to try to talk to the person about the manipulation. It's time to get down to the root issues of the relationship and figure out what can be done to help both partners get what they need, instead of just the manipulator. There has been an imbalance of power for far too long, and it's time to rebalance.

Unfortunately, not many manipulators are willing to admit their faults and sooner change their behavior. Instead, they'll do whatever they can to distract others from their faults, placing the blame on their victims instead. When this happens, the victim has to accept that their manipulator isn't going to change, and they must find the strength to leave.

There will likely be a desire to change the other person and help them improve their life as well. Not everyone will always be on the same page of their journey towards self-discovery. It can be hard to accept for some victims, but they have to realize that it's not their job to change their manipulator.

You can only help a person so much, and if they're not willing to change or improve themselves, it's not going to happen. Many people wait around for the other to change in their relationship, hoping their manipulation will get better. If a person isn't aware of their behavior and aren't actively trying to change it, nothing is going to happen in the end.

How To Defend Yourself Against Emotional Predators

According to Mark Leary, PhD., in an article published in the Dialogues in Clinical Neuroscience and the U.S. National Library of Medicine and the National Institutes of Health, "[i]nterpersonal rejections constitute some of the most distressing and consequential events in people's lives." This assertion may seem counterintuitive. After all, every day each of us will likely experience a very high number of social contacts ranging from long, complex interactions with people with whom we share a very close or intimate bond to casual encounters with people who are familiar to us to short, quick exchanges with strangers, clients, customers, or other professionals who together comprise the social universe we inhabit.

Generally, when we think about "distressing, consequential events," we think about catastrophic illnesses, significant disruptions to our financial or professional well-being, or the death or serious illness or injury of ourselves or loved ones. So, it may seem an overstatement to include interpersonal rejection in the category of events that we might consider "the most distressing and consequential."

However, Dr. Leary goes on to offer a convincing argument for the basis of this theory, an argument that may also help you develop both an awareness of how important maintaining healthy emotional psychology can be and understanding the importance of social interaction to your own personal and professional success.

Charles Darwin's The Expression of the Emotions in Man and Animals was an important contribution to theories examining emotional psychology and predation, and gave rise to theories of so-called "social Darwinism," from which popular culture derives its belief in the "survival of the fittest" ethos and the predominance of ruthlessness and cut-throat policies as the foundation of business success. However, the more important theme of these theories of human development is that "emotions [are] ... evolved adaptations that provide an advantage to survival and reproduction... In particular, emotions signal the presence of events that have potentially major implications for ... well-being— specifically, important threats and opportunities in [a given] ... environment—thereby causing the individual to focus on concerns that require immediate attention."

Furthermore, though we scarcely ever think about it consciously, emotions like embarrassment, hurt, and loneliness can often signal threats or challenges that emerge as the result of our complex interrelationships. Both acceptance and rejection are social responses to our own individual behavior.

When we experience the acceptance and approval of those around us, we are overcome with positive emotions such as confidence, and we generally are satisfied that we have somehow made the right choice or satisfied some standard that will allow us to move ahead in our lives. Conversely, when we are rejected, whether by receiving negative feedback in the form of a professional proposal that is rejected, a social invitation that is declined, or being entirely expelled by a social group, we may be overwhelmed with feelings of guilt and shame. Especially when we believe we have been rejected for reasons that are not defensible or justified, we may also experience a great deal of anger.

In a normal, healthy social environment these signs of social acceptance or rejection occur without a lot of pre-meditation or conscious thought—they are simply a natural reaction among groups and individuals within groups to behavior that either conforms to or violates the established norms and values of a given society. Yet, the degree to which our survival depends upon receiving positive social and emotional responses in the form of acceptance has a disproportionate influence over our ability to succeed.

For example, if you are a highly skilled attorney working in a law firm, you may reasonably expect that your skills alone will allow you to win cases and earn the professional and social rewards you would expect. And in a normal environment in which emotional psychology operates as a social function that is subordinate to and responsive to professional performance, this would be the typical outcome. However, in an environment that may have been thrown out of balance by emotional predation and manipulation, professional performance alone may not be enough to win you the recognition and success you believe you have earned.

In fact, if the dynamics of interpersonal relationships are thrown out of balance significantly, professional performance and skill may be a secondary concern that has been made subordinate to your ability to achieve social acceptance and approval. And if the decisions about who receives social acceptance and approval are made by emotional predators, all of your professional skills and accomplishments may be regarded as a liability. So, an emotional predator can control you and hurt you by placing you in a position of inferiority and making you a captive audience in a social trap that you may not have the skills from which to extricate yourself.

Furthermore, social interactions and interrelationships are complex and difficult enough to manage in a natural setting. The contemporary environment is host to an entire complex apparatus of unprecedented developments in the form of social media, email, mobile phone technology, video conferencing, and other forms of electronic communication.

In his thesis "Emotion in Social Media," Dr. Galen Panger, a graduate of U.C. Berkeley's School of Information Management Systems, has identified certain parameters in his effort to determine whether the emotional psychology of social media users differs from the emotional psychology that characterizes people engaged in normal daily interactions.

According to his study, users of Facebook and Twitter did not display extreme or detrimental effects indicating that the social isolation caused by these new media has led to an increased development in antisocial personality disorder. However, he did establish that depending on the social media forum, users may tend to be more or less emotionally positive or negative. Specifically, Facebook posts were overwhelmingly characterized by positive emotional overtones, while Twitter posts tended to have a more negative tone.

Conversely, because Facebook posts tended to celebrate individual attributes in an emotionally positive and affirmative tone, Facebook users generally experienced more aggravation of negative emotions like jealousy and anger, while the negative town of Twitter posts worked to cure feelings of frustration and anger among users of the forum.

However, the study did not focus on one crucial element. The use of social media is itself an anomalous and unprecedented development in the evolution of human relationships and generally occurs when social media users are in social isolation. All true scientific studies must have a control group, but this study lacks one. The control group for any valid study of human psychology and emotion must be a natural environment devoid of technological interventions.

Although Dr. Panger's study established that there may

be less variance or distortion among social media users when compared to each other, it uses environments largely regulated by technological communication as the default. The study does not address either how these disrupted environments compare to the human social and emotional psychology in non-technological environments, nor does it consider how technological communications devices and social media may enhance the ability of social and emotional predators to work in isolation, essentially unsupervised, to assemble profiles of their potential victims and create social personas that may strengthen their ability to succeed.

Thus, understanding the importance of emotional psychology and the presence of emotional predators is important for two fundamental reasons—our natural tendency is to seek social approval and acceptance, and our ability to succeed personally and professionally depends on maintaining an environment in which social rewards are distributed according to established norms. When this environment is skewed, whether in our own personal sphere of influence or in the larger professional or social environment in which we work or live, we lose the ability to fend for ourselves and sustain our own well-being. Upsetting this balance is precisely the goal of the social and emotional predator.

As a result, looking for signs of emotional and social manipulation in an effort to avoid such entanglements, and understanding how to respond and recover in the event we are caught off guard, are more than just refinement and sophistication; they are necessary skills for surviving and thriving in a world that has been dramatically altered and thrown off-balance in recent years.

Tips for Reading and Analyzing People

Overview: The Real Vampires

The most important step in recognizing the presence of a social or emotional predator is maintaining an awareness of the basic psychology of all emotional predators—whether they exhibit symptoms of psychopathy, Machiavellianism, or narcissism. Even if someone's behavior is not disruptive enough to be considered a sign of serious mental illness, anyone whose relationships depend upon their ability to emotionally manipulate others should be considered as potentially dangerous to your personal or professional safety and well-being.

This is because it is neither possible nor advisable to

conduct a full-scale psychological analysis of everyone with whom you come into contact and because social and emotional predators' main skill set involves defeating efforts at detection.

All emotional predators share some common traits. As a result of some type of congenital psychological impairment at birth, as a result of some type of very serious emotionally or psychologically traumatic experience or series of experiences at a very young age, or as a result of some combination of these factors, emotional predators uniformly lack the ability to develop genuine emotional attachments with other people, to develop any deep, genuine feelings of warmth, to appreciate or value the feelings, thoughts, or rights of other people, or to develop any sense of respect for the principles and laws that govern society.

Furthermore, because these predatory individuals have learned from a very young age to live, survive, and even achieve high levels of success despite these serious psychological problems, they are unable to regard their condition as abnormal. They may regard their compromised psychological state as equal to or superior to a normal, healthy psychological state.

The second primary component common to all forms of predatory psychology follows from the first. Predators are unable to live like people who are not psychologically damaged. They are unable to form lasting, meaningful relationships, they are unable to find satisfaction in the daily routines and habits of life, and they are unable to see any value in the pursuit of traditional professional, personal, or academic goals.

Predators must live in a world that is not designed to serve their needs. As a result, the only feelings they are ever likely to develop toward so-called "normal" people are feelings of rage, jealousy, and hatred because they cannot ever have or do or experience the normal joy, happiness, and fulfillment that psychologically healthy people may take for granted.

Thus, when an emotional predator approaches you, there is a lot to consider. First, because predators have become very good at finding ways to live and hide their deficiencies, you may not realize that the person you are talking to is an emotional or social predator.

Second, people with healthy psychology can quite easily communicate with each other the reason they have made contact through basic conversation. However, a social or emotional predator cannot ever actually feel any genuine emotions and never really has any value for the goals and objectives you may consider important. They are always performing because they are not capable of living any other way. So, when predator begins a conversation with you, it may seem normal on the surface, but the motivations will also be devious and treacherous, and likely the only reason they have started a conversation is to establish trust and begin mining you for information.

Third, the goal of all predators is the same. You may likely regard your personal life and your professional career as your source of happiness and fulfillment, and your motivations may range from professional ambition to altruism and selflessness. But the predator can find happiness and fulfillment one way only—by destroying your happiness, your success, and even you. Because you have something the predator can never have, you are a constant reminder of his or her own damaged and compromised psychological makeup. Yet, predators, too, need to find some type of fulfillment and satisfaction, so they can relieve themselves of what would otherwise be an existence filled with unending boredom and pain.

Through a process of tortured and impaired evolution, the predator has learned to mimic your pursuit of happiness and fulfillment. However, because your avenues to success are off limits to predators, they have established a new route—controlling you in an effort to inflict pain, abuse, and damage on you. Thus, whereas you may feel guilt when you hurt someone, the predator feels joy and glee and relief. Your path to success is professional, academic, and personal accomplishment. The predator's path to success ids the destruction and abuse of others. Regardless of the specifics of how these character defects and psychological impairments manifest themselves, all emotional and social predators share the same basic psychological profile.

Early Signs That You Are Dealing with a Predator

By now, we have examined the foundations of dark psychology, the psychological profiles that make up the Dark Triad, typical forms of manipulation in relationships, and how manipulation has manifested itself in society's institutions.

First, remember that simply because you are not currently in a personal or professional relationship that could be defined as manipulative does not mean that you are free of all danger and concern. Predators have had to learn the hard way to live and achieve success using cold and calculating psychology from which they truly do not ever get any rest.

Imagine being injured in a serious accident and losing the use of one or more of your limbs—regardless of how much you would prefer to have the use of that limb back, you will be forced to find some way to adapt. Emotional predators do the same thing. But because their injuries are invisible, and because of the competitive nature of the business world, they sometimes hold an advantage over us if we fail to maintain vigilance.

Emotional predators can blend into the normal landscape because it is easy for them to go through the motions of daily living. They truly do not care if things don't work out because they have no value for their relationships or the things that society has established as having value.

Consider that the serial killer Ted Bundy worked on a crisis hotline while he stalked and murdered young women. He appeared successful, outgoing, handsome, and well-adjusted, but was not. Or consider that the serial killer John Wayne Gacy, who murdered and buried in the crawl space beneath his home almost 40 young men and boys, spent his days running a construction business, held fundraisers for local political leaders, and entertained sick children.

It may seem nauseating, especially with these extreme and dramatic examples, but for the emotional predator, important responsibilities in society are less a source of personal and professional satisfaction and fulfillment and more a perfect cover for their predatory addiction. As a result, you may find it helpful to develop some habits that will help you learn to identify some of the telltale signs of emotionally predatory behavior.

Mind Control Methods

Now, you have seen just how critical persuasion can be in several different contexts. At this point, it is time to start seeing the techniques that you can use to persuade other people. Remember, persuasion is all about being clear about what you are asking for. However, on the other hand, it is also about convincing people to do what you want. You need to be able to walk along that fine line without falling on either side if you want to be effective.

You will be guided through each and every step of the persuasion and provided with the reasoning that you should make it a point to truly develop these skills. Each has its own important uses if you are willing to put in the effort to learn them.

Principles of Persuasion

First, we will discuss the principles of persuasion. These are six different persuasive tools that you can use in order to convince those around you to behave in certain ways. They can be used on their own or in tandem with others on this list. However, what is important is that you remember that these tools are useful, and you practice them whenever you get the chance.

Authority

The first of the principles of persuasion is authority. When you seek to appeal to authority, you are simply trying to make yourself into some sort of authority figure. This is for a very specific reason.

Stop and consider for a moment—would you rather take medical advice from a random person walking down the road or from a doctor wearing a lab coat and a badge? Which would seem more convincing to you? If both of them held out a pill in their hand and urged you to take it, would you?

Many people would be willing to be treated by the doctor in the coat and with a badge. They are deemed to be an authority on medicine just because they happen to be wearing a lab coat and have their credentials printed out on their badge. The other person, however, is some random nobody, and even if they were to say that they are a doctor, you would have no way of knowing for sure, nor would you be able to verify what was being offered to you to take.

Ultimately, this is exactly the kind of divide you would see ordinarily—when there is an appeal made to authority, the one who is knowledgeable wins out. The one deemed to be more of an authority due to credentials or experience wins out in the end.

This means that when you want to appeal to authority, what you need to do is make sure that you find a way to make it clear that you are, in fact, an authority on the subject. If you are the car salesperson, maybe have letters and pictures from your happy clients that have bought cars from you and left fully satisfied after your help. Maybe you should pay attention to the fact that when people walk in, the first thing you want them to see is that you are qualified at your job. You may set up so they can see your diploma or awards, or you will make sure that they hear about it in the first few minutes of the meeting.

Commitment and consistency

The next principle of persuasion is known as commitment and consistency. When you are dealing with commitment and consistency, you are effectively playing on the fact that people tend to like what is familiar and expected. This means that people will always try to continuously follow through on a commitment that they have made, and the more often that they make that particular commitment, the more likely they are to continue to make that commitment with it eventually just becoming standard.

For example, say you asked your neighbor, who happens to be your coworker, for a ride to work. It is literally no inconvenience because you both travel both ways at the same time. After several drives in which your coworker takes you to work, it eventually becomes expected, and you no longer have to ask—you are simply waiting by your neighbor's car before and after work each day to catch that ride. Effectively, the first time they agreed to take you, they locked themselves into a chain of repeatedly being asked by you for rides and agreeing to do so on a regular basis.

People love to be consistent—it is valuable to be consistent, and because of that, people will usually continue to follow through, even if they do not like it and do not want to continue.

You can trick people into doing things for you with this same process as well. If you want something, such as maybe wanting your coworker to cover a shift for you, you may start by asking a simple yes question, such as asking if they have had a nice week so far. Your neighbor says yes, and then you ask if they will trade shifts with you so you can make sure that you are able to go to a concert that you have been looking forward to.

Thanks to having already begun to say yes to other things, your coworker is going to be in a state of mind in which he or she is already saying yes, so they may as well continue. After agreeing to a few smaller things as well, you may run into someone who is willing to accommodate more difficult or larger requests in the name of consistency.

Liking

This is perhaps one of the most straightforward of the principles of persuasion—all you need to remember is that the more you like someone or something, the more likely you are to feel like whatever you liked is valuable, and the more likely you are to be convinced in its favor. For example, you are more likely to do a favor for someone that you really like than someone that you do not like at all.

Luckily, there are several ways that you can make it a point to become likable to someone else. You can, for example, mirror someone until they like you. This means that you would be copying their behaviors as covertly as you could possibly manage, which may not be particularly secretively if you do not know what you are doing. Upon setting everything up and mirroring the other person to the point that they mirror you back, you should be good to continue.

However, if you are unsure how to proceed with mirroring or you simply do not want to deal with it, there are other techniques you can use as well, such as choosing to intentionally make someone like you. This is not nearly as difficult as it sounds.

Start by making some sort of connection between yourself and the other party—perhaps you make it a point to comment that you can relate to the other person when they arrive with their child to an appointment. You tell them that you have a child about the same age and that going back to work at that age is just so difficult.

With the connection made, you will want to make eye contact and continue to talk. You may offer the other party some praise or a compliment, meant to make them feel like you genuinely care about what they are saying or what they think. The catch here is that the compliment that you make has to be genuine, and you must mean it.

Finally, if you want to be likable, you must make it clear

that the two of you are on the same side. Perhaps you point out that you will both be working together toward getting the other person a car. Maybe you convince them that you will both try to solve their problem, no matter what it is, with them. This camaraderie set up then makes it less likely for the partners to worry about them.

Reciprocity

The next principle of persuasion is reciprocity. When you are appealing to reciprocity, effectively, you are working with the attitude that you will help anyone that helps you first. You make it clear that you are happy to help them if you think that they will respond in kind. This is not nearly as entitled as it may seem upfront.

Think about how, when a friend buys you a gift, you feel like you must reciprocate? This is intentional with human development—it is done, so you feel the urge to reciprocate when someone else is offering you something. This means that when someone else has helped you, you will be more inclined to help them when they need help. You effectively safeguard with your own altruistic behaviors to make sure that both you and the other party are able to receive in your times of need.

If you want to take advantage of this, for example, you

may start by reaching out to someone that you need help from. Maybe you want your neighbor to take care of your dog while you go out of town overnight. You then offer to do something for your neighbor. Perhaps you clean up his yard before asking him if he can take care of your dog for the day. You let him know that all he will have to do is let your dog out a couple of times, and things will be fine. After having been helped by you, he feels obligated to follow through and help you out as well. He agrees to take care of your dog during your trip, and that is one less thing for you to worry about over the next several days.

Scarcity

Scarcity refers to supply and demand. Effectively, the more regular or readily available something or someone is, the less important it is. You can often see this with material items—limited edition items tend to be far more in demand than the same item in a standard color. For example, if you really want that newest game console, but you want the one specific to your favorite game series, you are likely going to have to find it on a used sale site and hope that you can find it at a regular price. Otherwise, you will have no choice but to simply trudge on ahead without that particular console.

This is because the regular console is common. It is easy to attain and therefore is not particularly important to you, nor is it deemed as valuable as the regular one to you.

Now, you may be wondering how supply and demand can relate to persuading someone to do something. The answer is that you need to make sure that you are able to convince them that you are in demand. Perhaps you find that your partner seems to take you for granted. If you have a serious talk with your partner about how you do not feel loved or respected, and during that talk, you mention that you would rather be anywhere but there because it is so exhausting to live completely unwanted.

This should cue to your partner that you will not always be available—you are only available as long as you wish to make yourself available, and that immediately ups your value. You can do this with other people, too. Reject the first attempt to schedule something with you and say that the date does not work for you. When you get to a date just a bit sooner, you can convince the other party that you are worth the money that will be put into you. You want people to feel like they got lucky to get you. After all, you are one of a kind—treat yourself like it.

Social proof

Finally, social proof refers to the tendency of people to fall for peer pressure. This is effectively just a fancy word for peer pressure and involves you actively making a point to choose to defer to what other people are doing. If you do not know what you should be doing, you effectively decide to defer to what you see around you. If you see that your peers are dancing in a circle, but you do not know why they are dancing in a circle, you are likely going to just join in without understanding why, and that is okay. You do it anyway and never find out why.

When you want to use this form of persuasion effectively, you will just want to set up a control area. Do you remember why so many manipulators liked the home-court advantage? It is so they are able to manipulate their surroundings. You can do this, too. For example, if you want someone to do something for you, make sure that you ask them around other people that are actively doing whatever it was that you asked them to do in the first place.

For example, if you want to go around and collect signatures and donations for a cause, you would want to be sure that those around you are actively seeing that you are getting what you want. When they see that other people are signing and donating, they are more likely to do so, especially if they recognize names, or they feel like they need to keep up with their peers. Effectively, then, this works well to keep people in line just by maintaining the environment around them.

Rhetoric

Another series of techniques that can help you become more persuasive is the art of rhetoric. Rhetoric is the art to speak or write persuasively in an attempt to get other people to see things your way. Dating way back to the time of Aristotle, the ancient Greek philosopher, if you are able to form your arguments with rhetoric, you can make sure that you are addressing other people in a way that is compelling and difficult to reject or ignore.

In particular, rhetoric involves three distinct methods of persuasion—these are three techniques that are commonly used in order to make sure that the other person is likely to go along with your suggestion. These are commonly referred to by their Greek names of Ethos, Pathos, and Logos.

Ethos

Ethos is an appeal to character. It focuses on making sure that the one presenting all of the information for the listener is viewed as credible. If the speaker is not credible, no one is going to believe in what he or she has to say, which means that his or her attempts and techniques will be particularly worthless. After all, you cannot clearly convince someone else to do something if they do not trust you. This is essentially quite similar to the appeal to authority in the principles of persuasion.

Ethos primarily can be seen in advertising—when you are trying to sell something, you want to make sure you have someone credible be the one advocating for your product, and staying true to that, you often find that celebrities commonly are called in to promote the brands. Of course, those people are being paid for their time and endorsements, but the effect is undeniable. For example, imagine a local sports personality making it clear that he always drinks one particular brand of soda without fail. The next time that you are in the mood for soda, if you happen to be a fan of that particular person, you may find that you are far more likely to pick up that same brand of soda simply because your unconscious mind wants to emulate someone that you are fond of.

This works precisely because people admire others, and

when they do admire someone else, they want to emulate them. People naturally want to be like the people they look up to or admire in any way, and because of that, they will be more likely to make decisions based on those admired individuals.

Pathos

The next form of rhetoric that is commonly used is pathos—this is an appeal to emotions. This is effectively coming up with a way to establish an emotion in your listeners in hopes of getting them to act in a way that you want to see. You may make someone feel sad or guilty in order to get them to donate. You may try to make someone angry in order to make them act. You may try to make someone feel happy to encourage them to like whatever you are promoting.

Ultimately, emotions are so powerful precisely because they are meant to be motivating. You are going to naturally feel inclined to act according to your emotions simply because that is why they are there. Your emotions are effectively your unconscious mind's way of interacting with your body, creating emotional impulses that are meant to keep you alive. You may feel fear when you are being chased by a hungry mountain lion, or anger when someone threatens you—this is because your emotions are meant to help you survive, and when you are angry, you are more likely to stand up for yourself, or when you are in danger, you need to be able to act in a way that will keep you alive.

Logos

An appeal to logic and reason is the final form of rhetoric. With Logos, you are seeking to establish as much reason as possible that cannot be denied to do whatever you are requesting. You may point out the numbers and facts that support what you are asking for, or otherwise use studies that support your opinion. Those using Logos have a tendency to throw as much data as possible at the other person, hoping that something will stick.

How To Influence People And Human Behavior

Most people in society have programmed their minds to agree. In their quest to be positive people, they have programmed their minds to be so positive that their automatic answer to everything is yes. They say 'yes' to everything, without giving it a thought. They perceive that remaining positive like this makes their lives smoother and more straightforward.

There is another lot, however, which is the target of most conversations, who have turned their minds to say 'no' without thinking. They are the policymakers, investors, potential spouses, colleagues, bosses, and others. They form the bulk of the decision-makers, the ones whose help or approval you need to do most things. However, they too can be swayed to the affirmative side by the power of the weapons of influence.

Below is a brief description of each of the weapons of influence.

1.   Reciprocity

One of the basic principles of life is to give back what has been given to you. People return evil for evil and good for good. Although that is not a good mantra to live by (you ought to do good to those who do bad things to you), it helps us to understand persuasion. Most people will make an effort to repay you so that they are not considered ingrates, moochers, and unreliable people who do not repay their debts.

Reciprocity could work in your favor is to do good to others so that you may receive good things in return. Treating people with respect, issuing gifts, and doing favors for them will have you treated the same way when you are in their shoes. The fact that you were kind to them even before they could do anything for you also causes them to like you. When people like you, they are likely to side with you and show you're their undying support.

Therefore, if you want to do well in life, always be kind and help others when you get the opportunity to do it. You might need help down the line, and the people you helped will rise to the occasion to help you. If you want others to be indebted to you, go on giving some uninvited favors to them (they need not be tangible), and wait to see how they respond to you in the future.

2.   Consistency and Commitment

Human beings, all of us, are naturally stubborn. Once a person has made a choice or taken a stand, he is under both internal and external pressure to stick to that decision. Externally, he wants to 'save face' while internally, he wants to prove that he was right all along. The desire to be consistent is also driven by the confidence from formerly successful decisions. If you have had nine successes with your choices, you will be firmer and more confident making the tenth one.

If someone publicly commits to doing something, they are likely to follow through with the promise. For example, during fundraising, people commit themselves to give particular amounts to the cause. If you ensure that these commitments are made publicly, through speech or writing, the people who made them are likely to follow through compared to if you take their private words for it.

If you are holding a meeting and you require that the people stick to an agenda, before the meeting, ask them to commit themselves to the agenda, perhaps by raising their hands if they agree to what you are saying. If during the meeting, a person goes off the agreed items, ask them to explain how their points are related to the agenda. If what is being said has no relation to the agenda, the person will quickly fall back in line, back to the subject matter.

3.   Social Proof

While humans may maintain that they are independent thinkers, in many situations, they rely on the opinions and social cues of others to guide their thoughts, feelings, and actions. They mostly rely on peers, the people they perceive to be similar to them, for influence. If you asked someone why he or she does something, he or she will tell you that it is because other people consider it socially correct behavior. For example, if you asked people why they have to wed in the church, and not the house, they would tell you that it is the correct, socially acceptable behavior. This is what we call social proof.

The social proof principles are even more evident in a situation in which the people are uncertain about what to do. In a case like this, if you show them what others like them are doing, they will more likely take the same action, without pausing to consider whether it is the proper decision to make or not.

One positive application of the social proof principle is in marketing through product endorsements. Product marketers get you to start consuming something or to use more of it, by showing you an ad featuring someone, possibly a celebrity, consuming the product.

Whenever you apply the social proof concept to convince an individual to do something, ensure that you let him or her see that many other people in a similar position are doing it, or they would be willing to do it. The more alike the two groups of people are, the better your chances of success. For example, if you want to convince a girl that you have been dating to marry you, show her how people of her age, her friends, in particular, have been married, or are about to get married. Your girlfriend will not want to be the odd one out, and will likely say 'yes' to your marriage proposal.

When it comes to social proof, it only takes one first person to take action to open its power.

4.   Liking

People are more inclined to be kind and to like the people who like them back, those they consider their friends. This is what the principle of liking is about, and its application is equally simple.

One way to get people to like you is to find common

ground with them. Perhaps you can connect with them based on your shared hobbies and interests. If you do, you will have solid ground from which you can build. For this reason, you need to be observant of the people you interact with, and see if you can pick up on some cues that could help you establish some common ground. You may find that you have the same personality traits, background, opinions, and lifestyle. Typically, people say 'yes' to requests from people they like.

Another way to get people to like you is to praise them. This could be genuine praise or flattery because some people are suckers for flattery, even when they know downright that it is not the entire truth. Praise and compliments make people feel good about themselves, and they show kindness and appreciation to those giving it. As you vow to charm the pants out of your audience, be careful not to overdo it. For example, when you go down the flattery road, don't make it so flatly apparent that you are lying or the plan could go the other way.

5.   Authority

If people consider you an expert in a particular field, they are more likely to refer to you for advice and information. They do this because they perceive that an expert will provide a shortcut to good decisions that they would take too long to make by themselves. If you are considered an authority in a particular field, it will serve you best if you would establish yourself as having that expertise and credibility. Some people take up titles, establish themselves as brands, acquire possessions and do many other things that would reaffirm their authority.

Many people miss the opportunity to be considered authority figures in their fields because they assume that people will automatically identify their expertise. They leave it up to the interpretation of those around them, but the result is that they are often overlooked.

There are many ways you can establish your authority in a particular field. One of the quickest easiest ways is to display your awards, credentials, and certificates in your office or at your workplace so people can easily see your rich background. Unfortunately, there are circumstances where this is not an option. Another way to establish authority is to mention your credentials as you introduce yourself to people, whether speaking to a large audience or having a one-on-one conversation with individuals.

Take every opportunity to let others know of your expertise; you could end up receiving honor, recognition, and payment for your services.

6.   Scarcity

Scarcity creates value, following the primary supply and demand rules. You can use the scarcity principle to persuade others by limiting your time and availability, which will create a sense of scarcity.

How your present opportunities to people matters also. The language of loss, one that demonstrates the value that you stand to lose, rather than gain, makes your message more compelling.

Another approach is to create an exclusivity impression. You do this by limiting access to particular services, information, facilities, and other like items (most of which are scarce), to create a sense of exclusivity. Exclusivity is translated as privilege or favor, and it increases the value of what you are offering.

With the six principles above, you have in your hands the weapons of influence. Therefore, try to take up the loss language, limited offers, scarcity, and exclusivity, among other techniques, to convince people of your high value, and that of the things you have to offer.

Create Certainty

When there is no sense of certainty in a situation, going forward with it, or being bothered about it makes no sense at all. Why bother, in the first place, if the results won't be favorable? The lack of certainty causes paralysis. It causes people to brush off or abandon great projects and ideas, and if they have to do it, they do things half-heartedly, making it impossible to achieve optimal results.

Certainty paves the way for action. It builds confidence. When you are sure about what you want, and the road to get there, there will be nothing to stop you from pursuing what you want. You will have clarity of vision and of the things you need to do to achieve it.

Certainty, especially about things you intend to do or achieve in the future, is built from past successes. You look at the past and see what you were able to do or achieve, and have faith that you will have the same results in the future. Present success is determined by weighing out the current circumstances to see whether they are favorable.

Overall, having a sense of certainty is life-changing and powerful. However, if you give room to fear and doubt, you will become an enemy to all of life's possibilities. Fear and doubt limit your movements and cause you to settle for less. The result is underachievement in all your endeavors, and you end up becoming just an average person.

If instead of fearing, you courageously march and conquer the obstacles to your success, know that you have begun your journey to high achievements that will in turn breed self-assuredness and certainty in you so that you can achieve even better than you already have. As you can see, confidence leads to more success, while fear and doubt lead to failure and greater failure.

Henry Ford said, "If you think you can, you will. If you think you can't, you won't." It all begins in the mind.

When people are certain about the future, they say they have faith. Faith is the belief that something will materialize, even though at the moment, it has not. Faith also gives you the certainty that something that you believe exists does. For example, people believe in the existence of God even if they have not met him, while others believe in the presence of ghosts despite not having seen one.

For you to see any change in your life, from having a new job, improving your grades at school, dating a new person or enjoying improved health, you must have a sense of certainty first. Whatever you believe you can have, you are confident you can have. If you give room to doubt, the uncertainty will force you to give up on your dream or cause you to perform dismally.

How to Build Your Sense of Certainty

1.   Examine Your Current Beliefs

To establish certainty in your life, you have to start from the baseline. Dig out current beliefs and see how each of them serves you. Do your current beliefs make you hopeful of greater things to come in the future? Do they motivate you to be better at what you do? Do they challenge you to reach for higher goals and ambitions? If they do not do this for you, you need to get rid of them.

It may also turn out that the majority of the beliefs you hold you adopted from other people. We tend to download some ideas and beliefs from those who brought us up and those we socialize with all the time, and most times, we do not stop to evaluate them to see whether they are true. As you evaluate and examine your beliefs this time, you will find that you do not even agree with a number of them, probably because you are now older, wiser and can form your own opinions.

Once you start changing your beliefs, you immediately shift from doubt to certainty.

2.   Get New References

The references of your beliefs are the experiences you have gone through or witnessed with your eyes. For example, if you have seen many people's phones get snatched from their trouser pockets, you will conclude that a trouser pocket is not a safe place to put your cellphone in. From there on, you will have a reference to this belief, and you can even confidently pass it on to others. If you have seen many relationships among college students breaking, you will have a reference that college relationships do not work. If you have seen and even experienced a happy marriage, you will have a reference that marriages create joy.

References serve as the foundations of either your certainty or uncertainty. If the references you now hold do not give you a high degree of certainty, you must rethink what you know about the issues at hand, and seek to find some newer, more convincing references.

3.   Become Curious

Things are constantly changing, and when you rely on old references to defend your beliefs, you might be mistaken to find that all that you knew before has been proven wrong. You see, we live at an age where information and things quickly become obsolete. The facts on which you based your beliefs a year ago are now outdated, you need to get newer information. Therefore, even after you have formed new beliefs and new references, be curious to know the latest information about different things, and keep readjusting your beliefs.

Emotional Persuasion: What Is?

Some people are always lucky in that they can get what they want at any time the need arises. Sometimes they do so at the expense of others, this, however, is achieved via access to the emotional bank. They can influence your thoughts or emotions to their advantage and leave you a victim and vulnerable. Emotional manipulation, therefore, involves access to someone and influencing them for information or any other favors through their emotions. It sucks and it is unethical once you realize what has been done to you. Do not get confused, there are two sides to emotional manipulation. There is an ethical and unethical side. What feels like betrayal is the unethical one. However, mastering emotional intelligence plays a barrier role to these manipulations and keeps you in a safe spot

Owning space

The main aim of emotional manipulation is to make you lose control of your emotions. It will involve making you stagger with emotions which on the other hand will make you even more vulnerable. Advantage will be taken and they will access you and get all they wanted from you. If there existed a lock to the emotions, I am sure everybody would have their emotions locked away and unlocked only to intimate relationships or where your emotions will be valued. To make sure you are off the steering with your emotions, manipulators will invite you to a place where they know it is new to you but familiar to them. This will keep you off balance, the new environment will give him or her the dominance and feeling of being in control. You are new to the place and the manipulator will take advantage of the window between adaptability and regaining control.

Your words against you

How you talk or react speaks volumes and emotions can be passed along. Manipulators like a talkative person since it is easier to access them due to the link provided; speaking out. If you are the introvert type or a conservative person it takes more effort to make you open up. Introverts would require tailored questions that will be well planned and will give you away from one by one. The manipulator makes sure the questions are aimed at the emotional state. Personal questions will open you up and you will start speaking with feelings, this is an indicator that manipulation is taking place and it is working. By asking simple and tailored questions that mostly are personal or involve something we like hobbies, interests among others will lead to saturation with emotions. A master manipulator will take advantage of the situation and make us of the questions to establish your beliefs, strengths, and weaknesses without you realizing it.

Guilt

Kind-hearted victims are easily vulnerable to emotional manipulation. Guilt will be used against you, especially if you are so sensitive you may end up giving in to their demands. Guilt will either make you give in or feel bad about yourself. For instance, you may both agree on something and when the time comes to complete the deal the manipulators will pretend to forget or even act as victims of your actions. By doing so they will be finding your soft spot and once they find it will be the target of manipulation. Guilt and sympathy will be served to you, if you are not strong enough you will fall for the play. They will influence you through that guilt since you will be under their spell and since you now believe they are the victims you will do all they ask just to make sure your 'victims' do not suffer anymore.

Positive and negative emotions

Emotions of sadness or happiness can also be a pathway for emotional manipulation. An emotional manipulator will play with your psychology, he or she will show you that what you might be going through is nothing compared to what they have going on in their lives. By doing this, they try to exalt you and win your trust. If you fall for that and believe there are more needy people than you in the world then you will loosen up and think that you are selfish. You will no longer focus on your big problem, rather you will focus on their 'big unfortunate events' since you will now feel pitiful. Once you trust them, then you give them a key to your emotional bank and surely, they will use it against you. Once you trust them, you might end up offering yourself to assist them, that, however, was their plan from the start; they will have attained their goal.

Anger

Anger is another emotion that can be used to induce emotional manipulation. Some people are natural peacemakers, they avoid confrontations and conflicts in all ways possible. Once a manipulator realizes you are this type of person, he or she will use anger, aggressive language or raise his or her voice or even drop several threats. These aggressive techniques are tailored just to make tick. The secret behind this aggressive approach is to induce fear and discomfort so that you can give in hastily without taking a second to think through. Once you give in to their demands they now get control over you and now can manipulate you in whatever direction or way that pleases them. They use this opportunity to get what they wanted from you since you will be cooperative earing to bring another instance of acute aggression.

Self-discipline and confidence

Being self-driven and confident is a very strong barrier to the effects of emotional manipulation. With the right mindset, you become less vulnerable to emotional manipulation attacks. Insecure and sensitive people are the easiest target for emotional manipulators. They are easily spotted and accessible, they put their needs behind those of others and are often feeling the need to please. All a manipulator needs is to be caring, sensitive and with an urge to help out. The needy part of sensitive people exposes them and the emotional manipulator will see it as a gate pass to influencing your thoughts, perceptions, and feelings to his or her advantage. With time the emotions break open and they are exploited easily since the manipulator was disguised as a caring and sensitive person. As the saying goes, birds of a feather flock together; the feeling of sharing the same trait will open them up for manipulation without their knowledge.

Surprises

Negative surprises is also another mechanism used to keep people off balance. When bombarded with the new unexpected news that comes with a limited timeframe will lead to panic. As you panic, you get little time or none to think of a counter move. They may be good enough to trap you with suggestions as they pretend to help yet it is a plan made to make you unstable both psychologically and emotionally. Once you become unstable and overwhelmed by the sudden change of events it becomes their opportunity to influence your decisions and any other emotion they are interested in. They may even consider making more moves that will bind your relationship with him, her or them so that they can utilize that window of opportunity created by the panic moment. You may not realize it since they appear to be assisting whereas they are using you for their benefits.

Criticism

Criticism is also a tool for emotional manipulation. The manipulator will say bad things of you, ridicule you or even dismiss you. He or she will make sure her mission of dismantling you succeeds. Once you have had enough you end up off balance and believe they are much superior compared to the inferior you. You will feel so down and their opinions will stick. Once you are in this state you are vulnerable. The manipulator will make sure you understand that you can never be good at anything no matter what you do or invest in. This will get into you and you will be emotionally distressed. You will feel hurt and not worthy of anyone's help. They will then pretend to have answers to your problems. He or she will give you tips and suggestions that are so genuine looking and constructive. Once these well-outlined answers transform you and get you out of it they threw you will worship them. Once they have your attention they can then make you do what they want or influence you.

Doubt

Doubt and uncertainty are also other forms of leverage in emotional manipulation. You will receive a silent treatment until you start doubting your actions or words that you may have used the last time. The manipulators will do this deliberately to stir up the feeling of doubt, once you give in and break the silence by acting as the cause of the silence treatment will be a good chance to be taken advantage of. This creates a window of opportunity and they will manipulate you.

Ignorance

Pretending to be ignorant of your duties will also get things done. You may want to do something but you want it done by someone else, let us say your spouse. She or he will note something is off and will try to make it right but you pretend to be good with it but since they know it has to be right they will do it anyway.

How to Learn To Use Manipulation to Your Advantage

Manipulation is something that we cannot master overnight. The closer you get to a person the easier the process of manipulation becomes. Making people fall into your traps and flow with your ideas making it seem it was theirs in the first place is a manipulative move. Getting things done efficiently would be our greatest achievement but when we get assistance and it is done perfectly, we feel more graceful and happy. With the power of manipulation which would take some time to master, you can swing things around to fit your needs and desires. Manipulation strategies will require some cold-heartedness since may involve hurting other peoples' emotions without caring. The focus is on what you can get and the method does not necessarily care about what your emotions are or what might be at stake.

Emotional intelligence

Learn emotional intelligence and practice it. To access people's actions and feelings, emotions make it easier. Emotions are able to access the mind; subconsciously and we react subconsciously. Unless you have mastered the art of emotional intelligence and self-discipline you cannot avoid an attack on the emotions' bank; the subconscious mind. The subconscious mind will act fast and without the awareness and consent of the conscious mind. This, however, makes the bridge to manipulation; the manipulator will now be in a position to access your feelings and play around with them so that you can tune to the song being played. Make sure you harness the power of emotional intelligence and be in a position to radiate the products of the same. Once you master that, manipulation will become a piece of cake and you will influence people's thoughts, feelings, and emotions to your liking.

Charms and flirts

Master the art of charms and flirts. People that like you without effort are likely to do anything to get noticed by you; the charming guy. Use charms to gain popularity and love from people, let people talk about how good you are and likable. To this, trait and image made out there add a touch of fluttery to spice things up; you will prepare lands that you can garden any time as long as you use the right approach to smoothen things. Manipulating people that have a crush on you becomes easy and when you keep your sexuality off the table and flirt, you will access control of people who are vulnerable. People with self-esteem are mostly people-pleasing and therefore when you show interest they will easily fall into your arms. Use this opportunity to make them work towards your goal or assist you in any way that pleases you.

Invest in self-confidence

Learn the power of being confident in yourself. People are likely to believe you more when you are confident in yourself and what you say. To win people overuse the right posture and words accompanied by a handful of confidence and magic will happen. What you say to them will not matter, your actions rather will be the target to scrutiny and once you win them over you will have their loyalty to yourself. Once they believe that what you do is for their benefit and you let it stick to them with a lot of confidence, they will participate even though it is against their desires.

Act

Be an actor, pretend to be something you are not so as to fit in. Learn how to use trust to open up people. Act needy and tell someone a very private and personal experience, they will be triggered to share theirs. It takes a lot of courage and trust to let go off of some of such private issues. Once you win the trust of the individual you are a step ahead in manipulation. The victim might not know the validity of the story if you act right and blend in feelings with the story and experience. The victim also might not be aware of the manipulation since the exchange of the experiences.

Empathy

Empathy will make people trust you since you seem to understand what they feel. Understanding people and giving them a shoulder to cry on is emotional support. People will trust you with their problems and insecurities as long as you maintain the relationship. Be a good listener and show care and understanding. The feeling of having someone by your side in times of crisis will make you do all to maintain him or her. Use the opportunity to make sure they tune to your beat. They might not realize they are helping out rather them it will be an act of kindness.

Apprenticeship

Working closely with a master manipulator will also get you a ton of skills in manipulation. You will learn by observing and apprenticeship. Theoretical knowledge learned sometimes proves hard to apply to the field. Therefore, learning the way to manipulate people under an expert as you watch it being done, chances are that you will become very good at it. You learn even more modified techniques that will not be covered in the theoretical class. Practice makes perfect therefore learning under an expert and practicing what he or she does will get you started. If you are this lucky to have a manipulator around make use of him or her to achieve the skills of manipulation.

Mirroring

Mirroring actions or postures of the target individuals may bring synchronization between you two.

Manipulators try to imitate your actions and posture both voluntary and involuntary ones. This will help open up the target individual and also show them that you are aware of their insecurities if any exists. Not only does mirroring involve the postures but also the words said. Repeating what has been said lastly with an agreeing tone will show that you were attentive and interested in the topic. Showing interest in what they have to say will make sure they do the same when your turn comes.

Conversational Skills Techniques

Do you wish that you could ever have a conversation with a person that you have never met before and they automatically like you?

Take a moment to think about people in your life who seem to always bring the best out of you whenever you have a conversation with them. You feel comfortable talking with them and you could continue talking with them forever. They could be somebody that you have known your whole life or somebody you have just met, but the conversation flows naturally and smoothly.

If you wish you could have this natural ability, don't worry. There are ways to give you this ability. You can be in control of a conversation and gain the interest of others. Now, while I may use the word control, I don't mean that you are the one constantly talking and "controlling" everything. I simply mean that you know how to work a conversation so that it continues flowing naturally. The most important factors in a good conversation are active listening, show curiosity, and keeping the sarcasm to a minimum.

But to give you a good start, here are a few conversation tips:

1.   Make the conversation about the other person.

Have you ever had the misfortune of sitting through a conversation with somebody who went on and on about something that you didn't have the slightest interest in? You likely felt wiped out by the end of the conversation and it probably felt like they were talking to their self. They are oblivious to the idea that you might not be interested in what they like.

The best conversations tend to be the ones that show an interest in the listener, their interest, and their world. Most people like to talk about their self. Take the time to ask them an open-ended question about something that you may have noticed. If you make sure that you give them positive feedback or a sincere compliment, you will have made a great start. Conversationalists are sincerely interested in other people, take the time to notice things, and use that information to fuel and start their conversations.

2.   Take the conversation deeper.

Think about the people in your life that you are most willing to open yourself up to and share things with them. What about them makes you comfortable disclosing personal things that you wouldn't typically tell others?

More than likely, they always make eye contact and they make you feel as if you are getting their full attention. Pay attention to expressions that they make. Notice how they are completely with you not only what they say but in their facial expressions. They look happy when you share something that you are excited or happy about. They will look solemn when you share something that is sad. You are able to feel that they are completely into everything you are saying.

If trying to emulate what they do seems unnatural, continue to practice this and push yourself until you have learned how to. You will start to notice that other people will react differently when talking with you.

3.   Ask them good questions.

You can get other people to share more by showing them that you are interested by asking them questions. This will help the conversation to move deeper. Some good questions are asking them how they feel or think about something that they have been talking about. If you have had a conversation with this person before, bring up something from the last conversation. More than likely, if they bring up something, it is an interest and importance. Take a moment to think about other areas that are connected to the interests you know they have and what they might like to talk about.

4.   Take into consideration the time and space.

Don't bring a conversation beyond pleasantries unless you know that you have time to listen to the person. Places that are loud with a lot of other people aren't the best to get into a good conversation. To have a good conversation, you need a slow and relaxed environment without a bunch of pressure and distractions. Coffee shops are good for conversations. Sports bars aren't.

Show Curiosity

Having a real conversation means that you have created a space for understanding. Real conversations give you a place for learning, and it helps to promote the deepening and nurturing of relationships. The most important of all is that real conversations feed our souls in ways that many other things can't.

So, improving your ability to grow, maintain, and create real conversations is a skill that needs to be practiced, whether you are coming from it as a friend, spouse, child, colleague, or parent. One habit that can help you to nurture a real conversation in any area of your life is curiosity.

Curiosity tends to be associated with children or highly creative adults. But curiosity is an important and fundamental quality that is needed for anybody interested in lifelong learning. There are four areas in conversations that curiosity helps with.

1.   When curious, we ask questions.

Alright, who are the most curious humans on Earth? Kids. What is that they do ad nauseam? Ask questions. What is it that will keep interactions with others from developing into a conversation? No questions.

When you have a conversation and you say something and they say something but no questions are asked, you might experience an exchange, but it doesn't go much deeper than that, does it? If you really want to stimulate the conversation, don't just create points and opinions, instead create questions about things that you would like to learn. If you ever start feeling like you are talking too much, shift the conversation and ask them a question.

2.   When curious, we listen for the answers.

Asking questions may be important, but having a barrage of questions thrown at you can feel like an inquisition. What takes us from an inquisition to a conversation is that after you ask a question, shut up, and listen. If you really want to learn the answer, you will listen for their response because you want to know. The main reason why real conversations are able to improve relationships is that they require a person to actively listen.

3.   When curious, we are interested.

Curiosity is what drives interest. Think about classes you did well in while in school and those you didn't. What was the difference? My guess is you found some interesting and others, not so much. Being interested makes you want to learn more.

This happens with conversations as well. When you are actually interested in the conversation, asking questions, and listening for their answers get easier.

4.   When curious, we want to learn.

When you are ready to learn, you put yourself in a place to engage in conversation for the purpose of learning, not just feeling like you have to get through it.

With these four things; questions, listening, interest, and

a desire to learn, you can create a conversation and get all of the benefits from it.

Active Listening

Listening is one of the most important things you can do. How well you are able to listen can impact your life in many areas. Since we listen so much, you would think that we are amazing at it. Actually, most people aren't, and research suggests that most people only remember around 25 to 50 percent of everything that we hear. This means that when you have a conversation with your significant other for about ten minutes, they are paying attention less than half of what is being said.

If you flip this around, it also means that when you are being given directions, you don't hear the full message. You hope that the most important parts are held within that 25-50 percent, but what happens if they weren't?

Clearly, listening is something that everybody needs to improve. When you become a better listener, you will also see improvement in your productivity, your influence, and negotiation. What's more, you will be able to avoid conflict and other misunderstandings.

The only way to improve your listening abilities is to practice active listening. This means that you are making a conscious effort to hear the words that are being said as well as the complete message that they are communicating. To do this, you have to carefully pay attention to the speaker.

You can't become distracted by whatever else may be happening around you, or by thinking about what you are going to say next. You also got to make sure you stay engaged so that you don't end up losing focus. To improve your listening skills, you have to let the other person know that you are actually listening to what is being said.

To fully understand the importance, think about a time where you have had a conversation and ever wondered if the person was listening to what you were telling them. You wonder if they understand your message, or if it is even worth continue to talk. You feel as if you are talking to a brick wall.

Acknowledging what a person is saying can be as easy as nodding your head or simply saying, "uh huh." This doesn't mean that you are agreeing with what they are saying; you are just letting them know that you are hearing them. Body language and other nonverbal cues let them know that you are listening and can help you to pay attention.

In order to become an active listener, there are five techniques that you should try.

1.   Pay Attention

Make sure that you are giving the speaker your full attention and acknowledge what they are trying to tell you. Understand that nonverbal language also speaks volumes. To show attention:

•   Make eye contact

•   Push aside distracting thoughts

•   Don't mentally think about what you are going to say

•   Avoid letting the environment distract you

•   "Listen" to their nonverbal cues

2.   Show Them You Are Listening

You can also use your own body language and gestures to let them know that you are engaged in the conversation.

•   Nod occasionally

•   Smile and use other positive facial expressions

- Keep your posture interested and open

- Encourage them to continue by making small comments

3.   Provide Feedback

Our beliefs, judgments, assumptions, and filters can distort the things that we hear. Being the listener, you are there to understand what they are saying. This can sometimes require you to reflect on what they are saying and ask a few questions.

- To reflect, begin your statement with, "What I'm hearing is…" or "Sounds like you are saying…"

- Ask them clarifying questions to make sure you understand things

- Summarize what they are saying from time to time

4.   Defer Judgment

Interrupting isn't helpful and just wastes time. It also frustrates the speaker and it prevents you from understanding the message. Let them finish their entire point before you ask them any questions.

5.   Respond Appropriately

Active listening is made to help encourage understanding and respect. You are learning new information. You aren't going to get anything if you attack the speaker or put them down in any way. Make sure that your response is honest, open, and candid. Share your opinions in a respectful manner. Treat them in a way that you think they want to be treated.

Sarcasm

Sarcasm, by definition, is "the use of irony to mock or convey contempt."

There are people in everybody's life who loves to use little sarcastic and passive-aggressive modes of communication. They think their sarcasm is well-meaning, but based on research, sarcasm is simply thinly veiled meanness.

Sarcasm is basically a way to cover up hate or contempt. It is a quick way to ruin a conversation as well. But why do people use sarcasm?

1.   Insecurity

When a person uses a sarcastic tone, they are trying to hide insecurity about something. Some use sarcasm or teasing to avoid confrontation because they are afraid to actually ask for what they want.

2.   Latent Anger

Sarcasm can simply be a passive-aggressive way to assert dominance. For a person who is upset or angry, but is afraid of bringing it up, they will use sarcasm to disguise their barb.

3.   Social Awkwardness

When people aren't that great at reading people around them, or they aren't sure how to carry on a conversation will sometimes use sarcasm to try and sound affectionate or playful. This is simply another version of insecurity, but this is common to hear at parties or other types of events. They will use it to try to lighten the mood; unfortunately, it will often have the opposite effect.

Sarcasm does not only tend to be hurtful, but it is one of the least genuine forms of communication. It's important that you watch the things you say. Sarcasm isn't funny because it normally involves hurting another person. It isn't going to improve a relationship or lighten the mood. There are other fun ways to lighten the mood, but picking on a person, and that is basically what you are doing, isn't going to help. You will lose a lot of respect if you constantly use sarcasm.

To be able to control and maintain a real conversation, make sure you remember these three important things: show curiosity, actively listen, and cut out the sarcasm.

Best Practices: The Optimization of Persuasion

Psychological Persuasion

In a wide range of ways, we face persuasion every day. An average person is subjected to around 600 to 625 advertisements each day, as per Media Matters. Meat producers would like us to purchase their latest products, and film studios would like us to see the newest blockbusters. Because convincing is such an all-round part of our lives, ignoring how we are affected by influences external to us is often far too simple.

However, persuasion is not only helpful to advertisers and salesmen. Learning how to use these techniques in everyday life can help you be a better dealer and increase the likelihood of getting what you want, whether you want to persuade your child to eat her or to convince your boss to raise her.

Because power is so valuable in many areas of everyday life, methods of persuasion have been practiced and experienced because of olden times. Yet social psychologists started to systematically research such robust methods only at the beginning of the 20th century.

Key Techniques

The ultimate objective of reasoning is to satisfy the intention of internalizing the convincing argument and to accept this new attitude as a central faith system.

These are all just a few of the most effective techniques for convincing. The use of incentives, fines, correct or incorrect knowledge, and many others are many approaches.

Develop a need

Another form of reasoning is to build a need or to cater to an established need. Such kinds of convictions refer to the fundamental needs of an individual for security, affection, self-esteem, and self-recovery. Marketers also sell their goods with this technique. Take, for instance, the number of advertisements that people have to buy a special product to be happy, secure, loved, or admired.

Social Needs Appeal

A need to be famous, influential, or equivalent to others is another very powerful persuasion tool. Television advertisements provide several examples of this kind of persuasion where viewers are invited to buy products so that they can be like anyone else or be like a renowned or respected individual.

TV ads are a major source of convincing because some estimates suggest that American watches range between 1,500 and 2 000 hours per annum for programming.

Use Words & Images Designed

Persuasion utilizes packed words and pictures also often. The publisher is fully aware of the strength of positive words, so many ads use expressions such as "Fresh and Enhanced or "All Normal."

Get "Foot-in-the-Door"

The "foot-in-the-door or" system is another technique, sometimes successful in making people follow an application. This convincing strategy involves putting someone to accept a small request, such as asking them to buy a small product and then to request it much larger. When the requester recognizes the low initial gain, he has his "foot in the door" and is more willing to fulfill the greater query.

For example, a friend asks you to sit down for an hour or

two with her two kids. After you approve the smaller demand, she wonders if you can just hold the kids for the remainder of the day. You may feel obliged to accept the great demand as you have already decided to agree with the smaller application. This is an outstanding example of what psychologists call the law of interaction, and advertisers often use its technique to support customers in the purchase of products and services.

Go big and then small

This is the opposite view of the doorway. A salesman starts with a great, often unrealistic demand. The person responds by denying, shutting the door on the selling figuratively. The seller responds by demanding a ton more, which is often conciliatory. People are often compelled to answer these offers. Since they declined this initial application, citizens are often obliged to help the vendor, fulfilling the smaller order.

Use the reciprocal power

Perhaps if people give you a favor, you will be forced to repay the favor. This is recognized as the mutual principle, a moral duty for others to do something since they have done anything for you first. Marketing professionals can use this phenomenon by making it appear that they are kind to you, such as "extras" or bonuses, which then encourages people to accept the product and make a purchase.

Create your negotiations with an anchor point

The anchoring prejudicial is a subtle cognitive prejudicial to negotiation and decisions. The first offer tends to be an anchor across all future negotiations when trying to reach a decision. So, you can help shape the future negotiations on your behalf if you try to negotiate a salary increase and are the first one to suggest a number, especially when the figure is a little high. This first number becomes the point of departure. While this number could not be met, beginning high could result in your boss having a higher offer.

Limited accessibility

Robert Cialdini is known for the six theories of control, which he first identified in his novel, control: the mental influence of persuasion, best-selling in 1984. One of the fundamental principles he defined was called lack or limitation of usability. Cialdini suggests that if they are scarce or limited, things become more attractive.

It is more likely that people will buy something if it is the last or if selling comes to an end soon. Of illustration, an artist could only do a limited print run. Since only a few prints are available for sale, people could buy before they are gone.

Please notice compelling reminders for spending time

The above examples are just some of the many convincing techniques that social psychologists have described. Seek descriptions of persuasion in your everyday experience. A half an hour random TV program is an interesting experiment that requires any single instance of convincing advertising. You could be surprised at the sheer volume of persuasive strategies that have been used in such a short time.

Persuasion Techniques that change the mind

The most successful people and renowned businesses use these eight persuasion tactics. Such persuasive techniques work on the unconscious and, if grasped and used correctly, will produce top-notch performance. We also analyzed and outlined the best tactics there for pleasure in learning.

Door footstep:

The door footstep indicates that you should negotiate for a tiny one before applying for a huge one. When you first ask for something small, you are committed to helping the individual, and the greater proposal acts as a reversal of something already agreed on technically.

Real-life Implementation: Tourist requests guidance. We suggest that they may get lost and need you to walk there. You agree with that more than if you ask the other question straight away. You lost a class and requested notes from your classmate. You then admit that this semester was very irresponsible and request notes for the whole semester. When you first apply for the tiny favor, the chance of getting the big one improves, a free ride on the notes of your classmate. The professor has not offered a refreshment, and you decide to ask for your feedback and why you have not accompanied by request for a redo. You have only failed. In such a scenario, rather than requesting a recovery, you're more likely to be successful.

Case study: In 1966, Jonathan Freedman and Scott Fraser, two researchers at Stánford, decided on a persuasion test to test FITD's effectiveness. One hundred fifty-six women in four groups were divided. The first three groups were called and asked a few basic questions regarding their household kitchen products. We called for their own kitchen cabinet to go and list their items three days after. Only with the second offer was the other group approached. There was an approval rate of 52.8% for the first three teams, while the last class had only 22.2%.

Door in the face:

The door to face is the reverse of the above-mentioned method of convincing. First, you ask for anything huge, with which you will not agree, and then ask for something that is, in contrast, easier.

Real-life implementation: You are asking a teacher in Advanced Statistics for your next mid-term. Oh, and until now at all, you haven't studied. The student apologizes and says they just have no time. Moreover, never before have they ever seen you. However, your follow-up application for your notes is allowed. You're telling your mate to lend $100 to you. You ask after the No, "can I have a minimum of $20?" A supermarket has a strategy of requiring a charity donation, before requesting the payment from the customer. Although most of our customers would not give money, the number of donations increases exponentially if the Store manager asks them to donate 100 dollars and ask, "How only about 5 dollars."

Case study: A study of the DITF technique to support retail sales. Case study: In the Austrian Alps, a saleswoman sold cheese to people passing by a hut. The walkers were decided to offer a pound of cheese for 4 euros in the first scenario.

The saleswomen first provided 2 pounds of cheese for 8 Euros in the second scenario, but after rejection, requested a pound for 4. Compliance rates vary dramatically: 9% for the first application, 24% for the second.

Anchoring

In most decision-making processes, anchoring is cognitive bias. For instance, how do you understand what "good" product is? You equate it with a similar item, and from there you determine. This technology has many various uses, among which pricing is most commonly used. If properly used, anchoring may be a strong technique of persuasion.

Real-Life Implementation: You want to buy a new car and consider an okay price for $10,000. You negotiate with the seller, and you can reduce the cost to $7,000. You go home with satisfaction and disdain, thinking about how much a deal it was. However, the actual value was less than $7,000 for the car. You will receive nothing lower than the initial $10,000 deal as an anchor, so you've only got a new job offer and an initial $2,000 monthly offer. It's about $2,200, which you settle. Once, you could become low-balled, as with the earlier example. Although an increase of 10% over the prior offer might seem attractive, it may still be less than your actual value.

Case study: Three separate payment plans were used by the Economist. A) 59 $online printing B) 125 $printing and 125 $printing and web printing. In a 100 MIT study, sixteen chose option A, and 84 chose option C. The experimenter then eliminated Option B and offered the same exam to 100 other participants. Enhance 8 Persuasion tactics to alter everyone's mind 68 selected option A and 32 selected option C in this case.

The takeoff is that people use option B as their anchor. Nobody really would choose it; it was only used to add option C value.

Commitment & Coherence

Principle: People are more prone to behave and believe regularly. You can use the initial promise to persuade an individual to do more for you if you contribute something little.

Real-life implementation: You purchase the same products time and again most of the time. How did you last try a new beverage or snack? "Will you answer me?" You remember." "Can you get me a drink out of the shop? You probably have heard that goal establishing will improve performance. "In comparison," Yeah, you could do, etc. The concept is seldom left out of a book of self-help. It is because of continuity that this is effective: you know more than once you write down this, it's what you want and therefore should strive for. Let's presume you're operating with an NGO, and for some reason, you collect money. You should ask the person to support the cause before asking for money. They would certainly respond favorably if the explanation is right. You are much more likely to receive contributions when posing such a request first.

Case study: A lot of websites now use the principle of consistency to make you register for their email lists. They usually read anything in their pop-ups: "Yes, subscribe to me. Free money, I love it!" And" No, I would like not to win. While it might look a little common, it helps to boost conversion rates.

Social evidence

Principle: This must be real; everybody knows.' Public confirmation is the most compelling tool for argument. It needs little to remember that there is a high degree of group thinking in most social groups. Somebody suggests a concept, and everybody goes with it—even if everyone opposes it. People just look at what their colleagues do and act in the same way before deciding.

Real-life implementation: You can consider filling the pot before beginning the change if you have a bare tip jar at work. Customers are much more likely to give feedback if they see an empty tip jar than a full tip jar, so I should actually be doing the same thing. There is a major chance that you could want a Facebook message if it has lots of likes, rather than a post that has none. Social data is the reason why most people consume cigarettes. Everybody cigarettes, and you ought to drink, even though it's safe and with an awful taste.

Case study: Many participants were put in a dark room 15 inches from a spot of light in 1935 in an observation made by Muzafer Sherif. The issues were then required to determine how much the object was going. There were different numbers both participants sent. On the next day, the same question was asked and put together. This time, the negotiations began, far from the prior estimates, on a completely different level.

Authority

Principle: People look to authority in any area or subject, so it can take you a long way to make yourself a link of authority.

Real-Life application: If they have been mentioned on major media blogs, many businesses or smaller companies place their "as seen on" icon on their landing pages. When, for instance, one business was on TechCrunch, that implies it's a big deal, since TechCrunch doesn't protect just anybody. 9/10 dentists believe the best one is a certain toothpaste product. It also supplies third world countries with clean drinking water. And heal cancer. In their landing page, organizations tend to discuss their predecessors. It refers in addition to large corporations.

Case Study: Where Stanley Milgram, a psychiatrist at Yale University, carried out several psychological studies that were sooner called Milgram Experiments. The research was conducted in three roles: experimenter, instructor, and subject. The instructor will ask the pupil, the hiring person, questions, who will be the volunteer.

The instructor would deliver an electric shock if the

student reacted correctly. Even after the learner "screamed pain," the experimenter continued pushing the teacher to use the electrical shock. In most cases, the teacher only followed the instructions of the experiment, despite being aware that he had caused extreme pain to another man. Even after their students stopped hearing any reaction and assumed that it was over, 8 out of 10 educators proceeded to deliver the shocks. The theft is that most people want to take control over someone, even to do something obviously wrong.

Scarcity

Principle: Scarcity is among the most widely employed salesmen and advertisers' persuasive tactics. People are more likely to want more of the low supply stuff. When you tell others that something is free only for a limited period or that something is in a limited amount, you would rather.

Digital marketing companies use scarcity by providing their goods once a year for a certain period while emphasizing the limited time that the product offers. Similarly, offer a discount, but connect a timer or date of validity. The greater the conversion rate, the more you emphasize how restricted the product is. Let's say that you are the salesman at the door. With this tactic of convincing, you can go pretty wild. You might claim, for instance, that you're just in the region that day or that you do a special promotion that is never to be seen. In other terms, at no other point will the consumer be allowed to purchase the item.

Case study: 180 participants were split into two classes in an experiment carried out by Luigi Mitton and Lucia Savadori. Next, an item was described that was meant to be rare, and the other was an ample commodity. The experiment reached the conclusion that it was less likely for students to select the good that they were told.

Ethical Use

The Freedom to Say No

If you want somebody to go along with your suggestion, they must first get the impression that they have the freedom to reject it. Request the thing that you want of the other person, and then remind them that they have the freedom to decline. For example, you might say to your acquaintance, "You can totally say no, but can I have one of those beers in your cooler?" Your nonchalant, non-expectant attitude will not only make the other person more likely to comply, it will also make them like you more as you display your ability to get rejected. They are likely to say yes because humans have a desire to please the people (and animals) that they like.

Performing this gambit will give the person on the other end of the conversation the impression that you do not expect anything out of them, and thus will more likely appreciate anything that they do give you. The ways in which you phrase this technique do not matter so much as do its implications. You can use phrases like "But please don't feel obligated" and "Don't feel like you have to." Communication scholars generally agree that only seven percent of communication is verbal, so a genuine tone will help this gambit's effectiveness more than an eloquently strung together combination of words will.

Reciprocation

If you hold a door open for somebody, they feel obligated to say thank you.

This technique takes advantage of the fact that humans feel obligated to help someone out in the future if they receive a favor or gift from that person. In many cultures, customs dictate that people bring gifts to the host of a gathering in exchange for their hospitality. So, you can make somebody feel indebted to you by doing something nice for them.

For example, charities often give away flowers in the airports where they solicit donations. The thoughtfulness implied in the flower giveaway lends itself to more donating. Amusingly, travelers often throw these flowers away shortly after they receive them. The charity workers then collect the discarded flowers, only to give them away again to the next flock of travelers.

One study conducted in a fancy restaurant in New York found that a server who gave complimentary candy to his diners received significantly higher tips than he did when he neglected to give out candy. His tips increased even more when he then let the diners choose a second piece.

So, if you want to prompt somebody to do something for you, first go out of your way for them. Of course, reciprocation works both ways; if another being makes an effort on your behalf, ask if you can do anything for them. You might just develop a friendly relationship based on reciprocal favors.

Foot in the Door

The foot in the door technique gets its name from the idea that you must step your foot inside of a doorway before you can pass your whole body through. Similarly, successfully asking someone to comply with a smaller request first will increase the likelihood that they indulge you with a bigger favor. Think of the small request as your foot, and the weightier favor as the rest of your body.

For example, one study found that a man, one at a time, asked hundreds of women for dates. All of these women were strangers to him. He received five times more yesses when he began his interactions by asking for directions or to borrow a lighter than he did when the date was his first request.

You might utilize this technique by asking a coworker for a stick of gum before you ask them to cover your upcoming shift. You might ask your professor to look over your report's first draft before you ask for a deadline extension.

Video games make use of the psychology behind the foot in the door technique when they "ask" players to complete easy levels before requiring them to complete more difficult stages.

I witnessed a panhandler use this gambit firsthand. As I was pulling out of the parking lot of a strip mall, I noticed an elderly man displaying a hand-written cardboard sign that bore a request for donations. I had a few quarters in my ashtray, so I took sympathy on the guy and reached across my car and outside of my passenger side window to give him two quarters. He thanked me, and then asked for two more! "I just saw you had them sitting there," he went on. It worked, as I sort of obliged and gave him one more before, I said goodbye and drove myself home.

This technique will not help persuade anyone to comply with wholly unreasonable requests. For example, asking a stranger to load your bulky furniture into a moving truck before asking them to buy you a car will, most likely, get you nowhere.

For a humorous take on this concept, see Laura Numeroff's illustrated children's publication If You Give a Pig a Pancake.

Mild Confusion + Reframe

Usually, when humans communicate, they carry expectations about the ways in which their conversational partners organize their thoughts into words. This two-step technique involves disrupting one's expectations of language and then reframing their mind in the moment of distraction. It is used to subtly influence another person while their guard is down as they work out the mild confusion.

Start by phrasing the next sentence in your conversation in a slightly odd manner. For example, instead of telling a potential customer that a certain item costs "five dollars," tell them that it will cost them "five hundred pennies." Then, while they try to figure out the more plain language version of what you just said, offer them a good reason for complying with you. For example, in that moment, you might say something like "I'm offering you a bargain." Individuals are more susceptible to persuasion while they are in a state of confusion. Confused individuals have trouble making sense of their immediate situation and are more likely to rely on others to make sense of it for them. By guiding their thoughts along after you mildly confuse them, you stand to persuade them.

Timing is essential for the success of this technique. If you wait too long after your oddly stated phrase induces mild confusion, then your conversational partner will be again fully capable of guiding their own thoughts by the time you get around to the reframing step. Give the reason for complying before they wholly make sense of your strangely said sentence.

Authority

Those with legitimate authority can persuade others to act, regardless of the suggested action's morality. To use an extreme example, Adolf Hitler persuaded his officers to execute millions of minorities in Europe. More recently, one study found that participants would willingly administer increasingly painful shocks to another subject if the researcher told them to. It did not matter how much the shock receivers screamed; around eighty percent of participants complied with the researcher's orders. Why? Because he was in a position of authority.

Even today, high-ranking military officials persuade their subordinates to kill people from other nations. Authority is an immensely powerful tool of persuasion that can and often does have fatal consequences if the wrong people exercise it.

Do not think of this technique's application as inherently evil. It has application in non-violent contemporary settings as well. Managers and bosses use their authority to persuade employees to perform at a certain level. Security guards use their authority to persuade concert attendees to behave in accordance with the venue's rules. If you want to better persuade others, earn yourself a legitimate position of authority.

Door in the Face

Not to be confused with the foot in the door technique, this gambit involves asking for a sizable request, and then asking for a much smaller request. One classic example of this technique in action centers on a man in a bar who wants other people to pay for his drink. He makes his way around the inside of the venue, asking every single customer to pay for his cocktail. Naturally, every one of them declines or refuses. When they refuse to pay for the drink in full, however, he presents them with a much more reasonable request: he asks the customer to spare him a few coins. Most customers oblige him, and the man pays his tab in nickels and dimes without ever using any of his own money.

Legitimizing Miniscule Favors

If you can make people feel like their contributions count, even if those contributions are largely insignificant, then they are more likely to contribute more significantly. After all, if a small favor puts someone in your good graces, what would a large favor do?

Use this technique to get people to do what you want. This technique involves making another person's miniscule contributions to your cause, whatever that may be, come across as meaningful and legitimately helpful. For example, charities often use this technique when soliciting donations from individuals and organizations. Their pitches include phrases like "every penny counts." Furthermore, panhandlers make use of this psychology when they hold up handmade signs that read "anything helps."

So, if you want somebody to perform a small task or favor for you, let them know how much it would mean to you. You might ask for help with your cooking routine by telling your neighbor "Hey, I'm super busy today and it would really mean a lot to me if you could let me bum an egg off you."

For example, after making your request in which you legitimize their egg lending, tell them "But I totally understand if not." Remember that subtlety rules persuasion, however.

Low-Balling

Low-balling is a persuasion technique in which one makes a request with the intention of adding additional clauses to that request once the request has been agreed to. For example, imagine that a salesperson gets a client to agree to buy a product for $9.00. At this point, the client is sold and committed to making the purchase. Before any money is exchanged, the salesperson informs that client of a $1.00 processing fee, bringing the total up to $10.00. The client would most likely agree to this clause and pay ten dollars. Why? The client has already settled on their decision to buy from the salesperson. Cancelling the sale would create a cognitive dissonance within the client. (A cognitive dissonance describes the uneasy feeling that one gets when their actions do not align with their thoughts and beliefs).

Anchoring

Anchoring involves comparing one thing to another similar thing. Salespeople will use this technique when they compare their product to similar offerings on the market, and then explain why the product that they sell is so much better. Customers perceive the salesperson's product as superior, and thus think that they must be making a relatively sound investment if they buy the salesperson's product.

Alternatively, salespeople and marketers anchor prices. To illustrate, consider the sticker price of a new car. If a new car has a sticker price of $22,000, it will seem like a good bargain when the salesman offers it to you for $18,000. The car may be worth less than $18,000, but it still seems like a deal because that price is anchored to the much higher sticker price.

How can you use this technique to get something out of another person? Anchor your request to a much larger favor that somebody else did for you. For example, imagine that you want an unfamiliar acquaintance to let you stay a night on their couch in the middle of your long road trip. Before you mention what you want, tell the other person about a recent time when a total stranger let you a place to stay for an entire week when you had nowhere else to go. Then, relative to your weeklong couch surfing endeavor, one night of hospitality will seem like nothing more than a mild inconvenience, if at all a type of burden. Of course, ethics dictate that you avoid making up stories for the purpose of getting what you want, but this is not a book on ethics.

Social Proof

Social proof refers to the idea that if everyone else likes or does something, then you should like or do it, too. Studies show that a man surrounded by beautiful women is perceived as more attractive than that same man sitting alone is. Most people would rather go along with a group dynamic than go their own route and implicitly disagree the decisions of a social group. You can make use of this principle in everyday life.

For example, if you have a tip jar at your job, consider putting a few bills and coins in it before your shift starts. This will generate more tips than will an empty tip jar. People think that if other customers leave tips, then they probably should as well.

Peer pressure works because of this technique's

psychology. Many young people feel obligated to drink or use tobacco because of the number of their peers who engage in the same vices. In many cases, these substances have been socially proven within the social group of teens and young adults who try them for the first time.

Scarcity

People can be prompted to take action if they believe that their opportunity for doing so will not exist in the near future. By placing limitations on one's opportunity to act, they will feel compelled to seize their chance before it goes away.

Think about the last infomercial you saw. Chances are, it included a line that implies scarcity. Infomercials tend to include phrases like "order in the next fifteen minutes to receive this bonus offer" or "quantities are limited." The truth is, these phrases carry little weight. You will receive the bonus offer no matter when you call, because it is always available. The infomercial's producers throw this clause into their ad and figure that if a customer asks for the bonus, then it was probably within fifteen minutes of the last time the advertisement aired on some station. The producers imply scarcity, compelling potential customers to make the decision to buy at that moment, rather than wait for the right time.

How can you make use of the scarcity technique in your life? Suppose you want to persuade another individual to go out on a date with you tonight. Imply scarcity by telling him or her that this is your last night in town. Or, perhaps you are trying to sell your car. You have the right customer lined up; you just need him to commit to the sale. Imply the scarcity of your offer by telling him that a dozen other people are interested in buying the vehicle. No matter your cause, scarcity acts as a powerful motivator.

Conclusion

In our world, we need to start to become more aware of manipulation. When you can recognize that someone is trying to control you, it will be much easier to stay out of their controlling grasp.

When you start to better identify manipulation, how it develops, and how it has affected your life, then it will only become easier to navigate without it. Interacting with others can include doing your best to avoid it healthily. However, stopping ourselves from being manipulated isn't the only important thing we will be discussing.

We will pay significant attention to how you can become a persuasive person yourself. Though you might have been hurt in the past by manipulation, or even damaged your mental health by being the manipulator yourself, there is hope, now that we can work towards a better future for ourselves. This is done by becoming an inspirational and potentially influential person.

Manipulation is dangerous, but when it is put in a more positive light, it can become healthy influence.

If you are able to be a persuasive individual and not only get what you want, but fulfill the needs of others as well, then it will become easier for you to be able to get the things that you desire the most in life.

Rather than always doing things you don't enjoy, being the "yes man," or letting people take advantage of your good nature, you can become just as influential as the people who have tried to control you before.

You might even be at a point where you fear manipulation altogether. Why would you want to do something to others that has actually caused you grief in the past? This kind of thinking is because we have only been aware of the negative types of manipulation. Not only that, but it is important to ensure we have the tools to understand how to get these things.

The first important step in this process is to investigate the personality types of manipulators, as well as the people whom they commonly go after. You may have heard of the common personality type, "Narcissist," a person who is only concerned with himself and getting the things he wants. Narcissists might take advantage of empaths, or highly sensitive people who are more concerned with the wellbeing of others.

After that, we will further explore positive manipulative personalities and the way that you can adopt some of these helpful practices in your own relationships.

Aside from that, we will also be discovering how our bodies communicate, the signals and responses that we give off, and what others might be taking away from our body language. The better you can understand influence through ways besides our verbal communication, the easier it will be to avoid becoming influenced yourself and to better persuade those around you.

After we understand what all of this means, it will be easier to learn and practice the rest of the influential tips that we will be sharing throughout the book.

Though it might seem easier to negatively manipulate those from whom you want something, the person whom you would be hurting most in this process is going to be yourself.

Always look for ways of positive influence so that you can mutually benefit both parties.

The question of why people manipulate others is still being answered today, with interesting answers. To begin this subject let's look at antiquity. People have been manipulating each other, according to historical records and the earliest bibliography, since the dawn of humans. From as far back as the first Roman emperors, people have been using tricks to play on simple innate human emotions to get what they want from others. By other promising false things, or playing on primal human fears, people have attained a certain great power, via using these simple psychological tricks to their advantage. The problems begin to arise when people use these techniques start to commit immoral acts on humanity, i.e. Joseph Stalin, Adolf Hitler. Individuals like the ones mentioned prior are the types who use manipulation out of personal conviction. The same reason can be applied to benevolent people, such as Gandhi, John F Kennedy. In simple terms, this means that a strong and rigid idea or belief is one of the main drives for them to use any means necessary to accomplish it. For example, in the case of Joseph Stalin, Communism drove him to exterminate millions of people without care. Or Hitler who killed millions of minorities all in the sake of a profound belief he conjured up; "Arian purity". Hitler, for example, gained his power by taking advantage of a country that, at the time was gripped by fear and extreme economic downturn. Of course, he seized the opportunity and took these fears and said to the people "if we do not do something drastic than these things will only get worse". This was accomplished by blaming people like Jews, or Jews who were Communists. He once said, "My beloved people, we must exterminate them, for a look at the disastrous state of our country; it has been caused by these monsters".

Everyone who gave Hitler the time was enchanted by his conviction and attention-grabbing aura. This was all done subtly; of course, it was a prime example of victimization multiplied by a massive magnitude. By telling the German people that they had been extremely victimized by both the world and the allies, which while true to a certain degree, he was able to assemble a massive force of angry individuals behind him. It is a powerful tool when emotions and time are aligned right. Now shifting our focus to the modern world in modern individuals who utilize manipulation such as abusive lovers, powerful men, salespeople, and agencies. Their reasoning for doing these things is the same in the past. See modern psychology, according to Maslow, states that a human being must sustain various needs through whatever resources they can get all to attain the highest state of function. This high state is something akin to transcendence, internal peace if you will. This is recognized as self-actualization. It is the top of Maslow's hierarchy, which is when a person realizes their own talents and potential. That alone is what will drive a person to achieve what they want or need with ease. Attaining a great worry free life is something that all people obviously and subconsciously strive for, but for some people, a missed wiring inside the human brain can lead them to take these goals much too far. By this, I mean that in the pursuit of pleasure, whether that be sexual or sadism, and wealth some people will do whatever is required to attain that goal, even if it means damaging and destroying another person in the process. Sometimes victims of this behavior tend to believe they can fix these types of people, or they themselves can change, which results in Stockholm syndrome.

Many real-life examples are because of this relationship and it can stem far back as childhood. This behavior can reach a point where it will even become self-sabotaging, leading to the individual destroying themselves in the goal of reaching something. In others, past trauma can lead to these behaviors. Take the individual who due to growing up in an environment full of abuse and violence that had to lie and be manipulative to survive for example. They may end up entering a romantic relationship and begin using manipulative tactics such as playing the victim or use intimidation to get what they want out of their partner. Out the simple virtue that it what was the kind of behavior, they saw growing up, so as a result, they have come to believe that this is the only way to do something since this kind of stuff has become so normalized to them. People who use manipulation, for this reason, are not people who can easily be helped. As their reason for using manipulation tactics is due to mental illness or past trauma, which is something that some people never recover from. Thankfully it is fairly easy to spot these kinds of individuals when you first encounter them. People who are overly needy of praise or need constant validation or who always sees himself as the victim in any situation they are in or straight up ignore you whenever they don't need you. These kinds of people have learned that manipulation can get them the feelings that they crave so badly with as minimum effort needed. As a result, ranging from things like poor parenting or experiences which validate these kinds of behaviors. As a result, they will be very unlikely to break these negative behavior habits and in fact, as a result, are more likely to continually do the same thing even if it destroys them. On the entirely opposite side of the spectrum, there are entities that utilize manipulation to gain the things that they want. News agencies, political parties, stores, salespeople, etc. Use the power of manipulation to usually further financial or power objectives that take priority first. Not too dissimilar from dictators or despots who did the same thing in the past. This kind of manipulation, while also more common, tends to also happen on a much larger scale. The way the news media or any reporting outlet, for instance, uses manipulation is by trying to only tell you what you want to hear as opposed to telling you the truth. They omit particular details about an event to invoke an emotion. This always has to be done subtly by only reporting on certain news stories or events. While the iPhone ad that may play on the same news channel will try and get you to purchase a brand new product by virtue of it seeming cool or flashy, and playing on the fact that people like things that make them feel exclusive or special while lastly getting into that innate fear of missing out on the big parade. The way a salesperson for an example will agree or reinforce any foolish or stupid preconceives notion a potential buyer may have about a car all in the desire to sell said car while in it neither malicious nor good. It is still a tricky tactic that not many people are aware of. This blatant unawareness is what these people feed on they know that most people are unaware of the fact that they are getting ripped off or falling under the spell of a manipulation. And as a result, they are able to continue using this kind of behavior to get us to buy their products no matter our life routines or the consequences. The main thing to keep in mind when realizing all of this is that no one ever thinks they are the villain in a situation, they will always assume that they are in the right regardless of the result of their actions. And as a result when you try and show them the toxicity of how they are behaving it is highly likely that instead of in fact listening and regarding what you are saying, it will only further embolden them and push them to move on to a better target. And get them to further behavior. This is the number one problem with the manipulation that forgets. Manipulators can be experts at presenting themselves as beautiful and engaging individuals. Dualistic thought it is the same aspect that allows them to reap so much destruction their ability to glib and charm you with fake promises and threats creates a perfect storm. While for some it may be trauma, the idea of gaining power or wealth that drives them to manipulate. For the very select few, they manipulate simply because they like to hurt people and like to see pain inflicted on them. This leads to a whole new breed of manipulation, which can be called psychopathy. Psychopaths are IMMENSELY dangerous beings yet they are few in numbers today in the United States. These kinds of people are extremely hard to detect which is a large part of what leads to the difficulty in dealing with them, how you can defend against something if you do not know what you're guarding yourself against. While manipulation has been used in extremely negative ways by quite a few people. With this I mean when manipulation is used in cases like negotiation or certain forms of policy making the net benefit can become better than the cost. I.E lying to an opposing county to avert a war that could lead to a large amount of death and destruction. Diplomats and ambassadors are created for this sole purpose and serve a great role for the nation. It is warranted, in spite of the good it can do. Numerous events and things in the world always require the correct timeframe and the precise execution to successfully manipulate others. Sometimes you may be worried about how others will view you or will change the way they think about you. This may be the case, however, you can always state your purpose in doing so and hopefully, if they are a sensible person, they'll understand. If they do not, you have to wonder if it's because of a lack of understanding and not wanting to connect or they had other plans which you foiled before they can enact them. You can never know what kind of people you hang around with. Your parents may have told you time and again "don't let others get control over you". There will always be those who are natural born leaders, who are able to bring others up and help towards a common goal. On the other hand, there are people who are deceitful masters and see others as pets for their amusement and tools to increase their gains. You can never know, only anticipate. If you had the thought "what if I am able to prevent any of this from happening?" you should know there isn't a way. It's only when you can plan ahead yourself that you can prevent it. If you ever need a reference to a book, you can use this.

www.ingramcontent.com/pod-product-compliance
Lightning Source LLC
Chambersburg PA
CBHW060312030426
42336CB00011B/1012